TIME
AND THE
SOUL

TIME
AND THE
SOUL

WHERE HAS ALL THE MEANINGFUL
TIME GONE—AND CAN WE GET IT BACK?

JACOB
NEEDLEMAN

BERRETT-KOEHLER PUBLISHERS, INC.
San Francisco

Berrett-Koehler Publishers, Inc.
235 Montgomery Street, Suite 650
San Francisco, CA 94104-2916
Tel: (415) 288-0260   Fax: (415) 362-2512   www.bkconnection.com

ORDERING INFORMATION
Quantity sales. Special discounts are available on quantity purchases by corporations, associations, and others. For details, contact the "Special Sales Department" at the Berrett-Koehler address above.

Individual sales. Berrett-Koehler publications are available through most bookstores. They can also be ordered direct from Berrett-Koehler: Tel: (800) 929-2929; Fax: (802) 864-7626; www.bkconnection.com

Orders for college textbook/course adoption use. Please contact Berrett-Koehler: Tel: (800) 929-2929; Fax: (802) 864-7626.

Orders by U.S. trade bookstores and wholesalers. Please contact Publishers Group West, 1700 Fourth Street, Berkeley, CA 94710. Tel: (510) 528-1444; Fax: (510) 528-3444.

Berrett-Koehler and the BK logo are registered trademarks of Berrett-Koehler Publishers, Inc.

Printed in Canada

Berrett-Koehler books are printed on long-lasting acid-free paper. When it is available, we choose paper that has been manufactured by environmentally responsible processes. These may include using trees grown in sustainable forests, incorporating recycled paper, minimizing chlorine in bleaching, or recycling the energy produced at the paper mill.

Library of Congress Cataloging-in-Publication Data

Needleman, Jacob.
    Time and the soul: where has all the meaningful time gone—and can we get it back?/ Jacob Needleman.
      p. cm
    Includes bibliographical references and index.
    ISBN 1-57675-251-8 (pbk.)
    1.Time. 2. Conduct of life. I. Title.
BD638.N44 2003
115—dc21   2002043861

Approx. 280 words (pp. 66–69) from the BHAGAVAD GITA, translated by Juan Mascaró (Penguin Classics, 1962) copyright © Juan Mascaró, 1962. Reproduced by permission of Penguin Books Ltd.

Project management, composition, and interior design: Shepherd Incorporated

FIRST EDITION
08 07 06 05 04 03   10 9 8 7 6 5 4 3 2 1

For Miles and Harlene

CONTENTS

CONCLUSION
"You've Only Just Begun"   **147**

FOREWORD

If you have picked up this book, gentle reader, because you feel starved of time, permanently harried, pressurized by obligations, comprehensively devoid of serenity, and so on—then be warned: this is not a self-help book. Instead, Jerry Needleman has written a *Self*-help book.

To clarify, self-help books consist of:

a. Forty-odd pages telling you how widespread your problem is, complete with reassuring anecdotes with names carefully disguised.

b. Seventy-odd pages telling you the life-changing benefits that will accrue to anyone reading said book.

c. Sixty pages telling you how the author modestly stumbled upon this ground-breaking IDEA.

d. Somewhere around page 178, the IDEA itself.

e. Eighty pages of predictable working-through of said IDEA.

f. Twenty-odd pages telling you how you can give more money to the author through various courses, spin-offs, self-help groups based on the IDEA, and so on.

However, this Self-help book explains why the self-help approach to our time problem is akin to rearranging the deck chairs on the *Titanic*. He shows that only a change in the scale of our thinking can really help us, and that change involves accessing our real Self.

He recounts an extraordinary experience he had in his teens that he says "was a taste, a forerunning, of the Self." And he explores this idea for the rest of the book.

The astonishing thing about his writing is that it somehow conveys the change of scale involved in a way that touches you at your core. For example, Jerry suggests some feeling experiments that I've never done before, and which caused me, for several hours, to experience my own life slightly differently.

So, frankly, this book is a bit alarming. Worse, Jerry stresses that what he has written is merely a first step in creating the conditions under which we might encounter our Self more often. He encourages those interested to pursue their Self through the great sacred traditions.

So, dear reader, unless you're truly interested in change, a self-help book might be much less disturbing.

John Cleese

INTRODUCTION TO THE PAPERBACK EDITION

The world is too much with us; late and soon,
Getting and spending, we lay waste our powers . . .
—**William Wordsworth**

The question of our relationship to time is both a mystery and a problem. It calls to us from the deepest recesses of the human heart. And it bedevils us on all the surfaces of our everyday life. At the deeper levels, in front of the *mystery* of time, we are mortal beings solemnly aware of our finitude—longing, perhaps, for that in ourselves which partakes of the eternal. But at the surface levels of ourselves, in front of the *problem* of time, we are like frantic puppets trying to manage the influences of the past, the threats and promises of the future and the tense demands of the ever-diminishing present moment. The *mystery* of time has the power to call us quietly back to ourselves and toward our essential freedom and humanness. The problem of time, on the other hand, agitates us and "lays waste our powers."

In 1997, when this book was first published, the uniquely modern form of the problem of time—the astonishing fact that the conditions of contemporary life are bleeding meaningful time out of our lives—had already begun to assume epidemic proportions. Almost all of us—including even young children—were being afflicted by this new poverty, this *time-poverty*. Awash in material goods, awash in new and ingenious forms of money and their ever-darkening shadow of debt, whipped faster and faster by advancing technology—and all the while telling ourselves we were better off than ever before—we began to realize, dimly at first, that we were no longer living our lives. We began to see that our lives were living us. And we began to suspect that our relationship to time had become so toxic precisely because we had forgotten how to bring to our day-to-day lives the essential question of who and what a human being is and is meant to be. We had lost touch with the *mystery* of time—that is to say, the mystery of our humanness, our being, our life and death.

This edition seeks to explore what it means to allow the mystery of time to irrigate our parched and driven lives. My fundamental premise is that the pathology of our relationship to time can be healed only as we allow ourselves to be penetrated by the mystery of what we are beneath the surface of ourselves—by striving, that is, to remember our Selves. Both the content and the form of this book have been shaped by this intention and premise.

How is it that as we grow older time passes through our hands more and more rapidly? Who among us doesn't now and again longingly recall some sweet passages of time when we were young children—the huge days and weeks of a summer, perhaps, or simply idle hours happily "doing nothing"? This sense that time is passing more and more quickly is, of course, a common human experience. But it may be that in our contemporary culture the speeding up—and, hence, the vanishing—of time has assumed uniquely frightening proportions. How often it happens that we come to the end of a day or a week or a month shaken by the realization of how quickly it is all going by! With a troubled, backward glance we wonder to ourselves: "Where was I?"

It is a very telling question and a very accurate clue to the problem of time in our personal lives—and in the life of the modern world. Where was I? Where *am* I? In fact, I was not there, I am not present in my life; *I* do not inhabit my life. And one can imagine the chilling prospect even of coming to the end of one's days with the same bewildered, anguished cry: "Where was I?" Is my whole life somehow passing by without me? That is surely what it means to say that meaningful time is disappearing from our lives.

We may say we wish for more time, for longer life, but this specific problem of the disappearance of meaningful time cannot be solved by having more time in a quantitative sense. A man or woman could live a hundred years, a thousand years, but if he or she was not *there*, not present in his or her life, it would come to the same thing at the end: "Where was I?"

It is precisely this question and this problem that has by now burrowed into the core of our whole civilization. The current of change in world affairs, in the patterns and mores of human culture, in the march of history and even in the biological and geological processes of planet earth seems to be accelerating in ways that are equally bewildering—when they are not absolutely terrifying. The boundaries and leadership of nations and governments seem more and more fragile, in many regions rapidly falling and rising and falling again under who knows what influences and causes. In the sciences hardly a day goes by without fundamental assumptions about the natural world or the human body being challenged by one "breakthrough" after another, resulting in a disordered mix of hope, disappointment and pervasive moral confusion. And as for the practical applications of modern science, it is no exaggeration to say that the continuously accelerating influence of advanced technology is more and more rapidly changing nearly every pattern of human conduct in nearly every corner of the world and within nearly every culture and every tradition of the world: in family relations, in sexual morality, in the meaning and nature of work, in business, in religion, in the arts, in the nature of childhood and the instruments of education, in the self-concept and despair of the rising generation, in the meaning of love—the list is endless. There is absolutely no corner or pocket of human life that is not changing with such acceleration as to induce a helpless numbing of our sensibilities—or else an agitated and often divisive, piecemeal activism that remains equally helpless, beating out small fires while behind our backs an inferno of ever-accelerating change throws its thousand sparks over the whole of the world and the whole of our common life.

But it is necessary to realize that technology itself is not the cause of our problem of time. Its influence on our lives is a result, not a cause—the result of an unseen accelerating process taking place in ourselves, in our inner being. Whether we point to the effect of communication technology (such as e-mail) with its tyranny of instant communication; or to the computerization, and therefore the mentalization of so many human activities that previously required at least some participation of our physical presence; or to any of the other innumerable transformations of human life that are being brought about by the new technologies, the essential element to recognize is how much of what we call "progress" is accompanied by and measured by the fact that human beings need less and

less conscious attention to perform their activities and
lead their lives. The real power of the faculty of attention,
unknown to modern science, is one of the indispensable
and most central measures of humanness—of the being
of a man or a woman—and has been so understood, in
many forms and symbols, at the heart of all the great spiritual teachings of the world. The effects of advancing
technology, for all the material promise they offer the
world (along with the dangers, of course) is but the most
recent wave in a civilization that, without recognizing
what it was doing, has placed the satisfaction of desire
above the cultivation of being. The deep meaning of
many rules of conduct and moral principles of the past—
so many of which have been abandoned without our
understanding their real roots in human nature—
involved the cultivation and development of the uniquely
human power of attention, its action in the body, heart
and mind of man. To be present, truly present, is to have
conscious attention. This capacity is the key to what it
means to *be* human.

It is not, therefore, the rapidity of change as such that
is the source of our problem of time. It is the metaphysical fact that the being of man is diminishing. In the world
as in oneself, time is vanishing because we have lost the
practice of consciously inhabiting our life, the practice of
bringing conscious attention to ourselves as we go about
our lives. All clichés about "be here, now" aside, the fundamental fact is that, in ways we cannot imagine, the key
to living the values we prize—freedom, moral will, com-

passion, common sense and far-seeing wisdom—depend on the exercise and development of the uniquely human capacity to free our attention from its "capture" by the impulses of the body and the imaginings and automatisms of the mind and emotions. In the world as in oneself, everything depends of the *presence* of humanness—in oneself it depends on the presence, even if only to a relative degree, of the Self, the real I am—and in the life of the world it depends on the presence of people who have and can manifest this capacity to be, or even only who wish for it and who come together to learn from each other and to help each other for that purpose.

To ask where are the *people* is to ask where is the soul of the whole of humanity? Where are the men and women of being and genuine honor? The metaphysical fact—and such facts exist; they are properly called cosmic laws—is that the vanishing of time in our lives is the result of the progressive diminishing of the inner life of people, not only our individual inner lives, but the inner life of humankind as a whole. Where are the *people*? That is, in the whole of contemporary life, where are the men and women who understand how to search for what is objectively good and true and who understand how to call the rest of us to that search and that way of life? Just as *I* am not present in my body and my life, so authentic humanness seems to be disappearing from the body and the life of humankind as a whole. Where are the *people*?

Some years ago I was walking in downtown San Francisco—in the financial district— with a great friend,

a learned Tibetan scholar who was helping some col-
leagues and me translate one of the most beloved sacred
texts of Tibetan Buddhism, *The Life of Milarepa*. My
friend had lived a long time in North America and was a
frequent visitor to the United States. He was a layman,
married and a father; he did not hold religious office and
was not materially supported by a religious community.
He had to make his way in the same world as the rest of
us; he wore neither the robes nor the social "armor" of a
lama or guru. One sensed in him the depth of Asian wisdom uniquely joined to the raw experience of the conditions of modern, Western culture with all its shocks and
temptations, all its psychological, social and financial pres-
sures, its tempo, its brilliance and its darkness. He was
outwardly and inwardly a man who lived in and between
two worlds—one an ancient, spiritually determined society and the other our own culture with its progressively
diminishing understanding of the being of man.

We were discussing the Buddhist idea of what it means
to be a human. One of the most compelling expressions
of the Buddhist notion of humanness concerns the rarity
of the event of being born into the world in human form,
in contrast to the other forms of existence that Buddhism
recognizes: animals, plants, denizens of hell, "gods," "god-
desses," "angels" and demons of all kinds. In the symbolic
realism of the Tibetan tradition human beings occupy a
uniquely central place in the whole cosmic scheme, precisely intermediate between the "gods" (who themselves
are victims of "higher" illusions) and the ghosts and

denizens of the lower worlds. In this central cosmic place, containing within himself all the impulses and forces of all the worlds, man alone has the possibility of working to escape from *samsara,* the endlessly turning cycle of illusion and suffering.

I was asking my friend about one of the most striking ways that the Tibetans express the uniqueness of the human condition. Imagine, they say, that deep in the vast ocean there swims a great and ancient turtle who surfaces for air only once every hundred years. Imagine further that floating somewhere in the ocean is a single ox-yoke carried here and there by the random waves and currents. What are the chances that when the turtle surfaces, his head will happen to emerge precisely through the center of the ox-yoke? *That* is how rare it is to be born as a human being!

In the middle of our conversation, I pointed to the crowds of men and women rushing by on the street and I gestured in a way to indicate not only them, but all the thousands and millions of people rushing around in the world. "Tell me, Lobsang," I said, "if it is so rare to be born a human being, how come there are so many people in the world?"

My friend slowed his pace and then stopped. He waited for a moment, taking in my question. I remember suddenly being able to hear, as though for the first time, the loud and frenetic traffic all around us. He looked at me and very quietly replied, "How many human beings do you see?"

In a flash, I understood the meaning of the story and the idea. Most of the people I was seeing, in the inner state they were in at that moment, were not really people at all. Most were what the Tibetans call "hungry ghosts." They did not really exist. They were not really *there*. They were *busy*, they were *in a hurry*. They—like all of us— were obsessed with doing things *right away*. But *right away* is the opposite of *now*—the opposite of the lived present moment in which the passing of time no longer tyrannizes us. The hungry ghosts are starved for "more" time; but the more time we hungry ghosts get, the more time we "save," the hungrier we become, the less we actually *live*. And I understood that it is not exactly more time, more days and years, that we are starved for, it is *the present moment*. Through our increasing absorption in busyness, we have lost the present moment. "Right away" is not *now*. What a toxic illusion!

It is clear that there is less and less in our culture to help us remember what it means to be a human self, to have being in our presence—inwardly to allow another, immeasurably finer sensitivity, another Self to "arrive" within and behind our thoughts, feelings and actions. To ask where are the people is to ask where are the influences, the reminders that can call us back to what we are meant to be inwardly—to remind us that without inner presence our life in time will pass us by as though we never existed. Where are the ideas, the art, the literature, the science, the religion that can call meaningful time back into our lives? Above all, where are the people who can carry to us such ideas, such art, literature, science and religion, people who show us by the quality of their own lives, by their actions and "emanations," that it is possible to live a fully human life within the very life we are obliged to live in this era with all its demands and constant change? Where are the people who demonstrate the metaphysical meaning of virtue and honor and love—that is to say, their roots in the level of our being, rather than only in words and purported rules of conduct?

In the few years since this book was first published, two major shocks have, each in its own way, made us more aware than ever of the metaphysical crisis of our common life in the modern world. The sudden revelation of widespread corruption in the heart of American business has come to us as a bizarre conclusion to and commentary upon a decade of neurotic consumerism and smoldering self-deceptive economic euphoria. As such, it has shown us something profoundly disturbing about the disappearance of character in the places of power and trust.

Of course, humanity being what it is, there has always been and there always will be pockets of ethical corruption in the corridors of wealth and power, but the present moral crisis in the top echelons of business seems to indicate a human emptiness spreading into the blood and tissues of our whole world. It is not that our society is suddenly full of criminals, but that people of genuine human substance are more and more rarely encountered in the so-called real world of practical action, such as the world of business and finance. Much of what is called white-collar crime is actually more a testimony to empty hearts and minds than to the kind of malice and cruelty usually associated with acts of crime. With loss of trust in business, however, there inevitably comes a deepening fear concerning one's own material well-being. The sense of the reality of money, which depends on trust, becomes more and more suspect. And with personal fear comes hasty action, and with haste and panic, however disguised, there may come the loss of the political and material conditions that protect liberty and permit men and women freely to search for inner truth individually and in community. The point is that without contact with our true human presence, humanness, and human time, are bled out of our common life.

Taken together with so many other signs of metaphysical emptiness in our present world—so much of domestic violence, so much of suicidal despair in our young people, so much of depression and the last resort of psychotropic drugs (whether socially sanctioned or not), to name just a few examples—it is hard to avoid the impression that spiritually and morally our society may in its own unique way be touching bottom. Which means, speaking metaphysically, that we are becoming acutely and accurately aware of our need. That is, our world, our society, ourselves in our common life, may be closer to awakening. We are stirring in our sleep. The shock of our human emptiness has been acting like the sound of a gradually increasing alarm that we are dimly becoming aware of as ringing in our very own house, our very own room, next to our very own pillow. In that sense, there is new hope precisely because the situation is worsening.

The second great shock, of course, was September 11, 2001, and the continuing unfolding of its consequences. Metaphysically, as well as politically, it was an earthquake. Like an earthquake, it brought onrushing America to a sudden stop. Like an earthquake, it compelled us to see our vulnerability, our collective finitude—might we even say our mortality—as a nation and a culture. Like an earthquake, it allowed us to experience feelings about ourselves and our country that for most of us had long been obscured by the momentum of feverish prosperity and consumerism. In that sense, it awakened us to the question of who we are and where we are going. It brought the nation, and perhaps even the world, into the present moment—very like an earthquake.

But, unlike an earthquake, what confronted us was not the immensity of the forces of nature and the earth, forces which bring all human beings and all nations and cultures to their knees, an immensity which in its heart our scientific civilization has been especially adept at forgetting even as with its mind it discovers more and more about the vastness of the living universe. What confronted us was not great nature—not nature, but *man*—the power in man of hatred, the awesome power of men to inflict death and horror upon themselves. Yes, everywhere in the world, everywhere in history, mankind has inflicted incomprehensible death and horror upon itself—in degrees and kind which make the complete story of the human race nothing short of a cosmic obscenity—the Jewish holocaust, the American Indian holocaust, the Armenian holocaust, the Rwandan holocaust—and on and on long into the dark night of the bottomless past and throughout the endless reaches of all the cultures everywhere on earth. Yes, man has killed man and has destroyed nearly every trace of the good created by genuine human beings for the welfare of posterity. So, yes, September 11 brought home to *us* the fact that evil enters the world through man and that through man, through the human being that we can see and touch, through the human being who is next to us, through the being with whom we grow our ideas and our feelings and in whose world we wish to move and love and create and serve—through man, through the human substance that is closer to us than the air we breathe—through man, through consciousness, through feeling, through religion, through ingenuity, through the mind, through the wondrous human body, through the magic of language, through the idea of god, through the dream of service to something higher—through us as well as to us, through you, through me—death and destruction not only enter the world, but they may and can overcome the world!

In this attack upon America, it was not just a fantasy of invulnerability that was exploded, it was the symbol of a place in the heart and mind, a protected place in which to search for humanness—whatever that meant. Yes, with September 11, America experienced what so many other peoples and nations have experienced through the ages, and in that sense its importance may of course be greatest only to Americans. But whether one knew or not, America was not only a geographical place, with its historical actions both astonishingly good and astonishingly bad—it was a symbol of hope. The hope of physical safety, yes, but also the hope of a harbor from which to seek the good for oneself and for each other. The murder of thousands may be but one more obscene act by an obscenely twisted mankind. But a knife into the body of the idea of America is a wound in the heart of the modern world—and everyone who lives in that world feels that, whether they say it or not.

I remember very clearly the 1989 earthquake in San Francisco. In the days following the quake it was as though the entire San Francisco Bay Area was remembering its humanness—as though almost everyone was remembering their Selves. People acted and spoke with extraordinary quiet and gentleness; they helped each other, listened to each other. There were no "angry cars," there were few harsh human sounds in the air. And, directly to the point, *time reappeared in our lives,* meaningful, human time. The clock did not race; the hours did not disappear; seconds and minutes did not matter. What mattered was that we were alive—we existed. Our houses were just houses, no more or less; our plans were just plans, no more or less. But we were there; I existed and *you* existed. People had reappeared in the world. And when people appeared, time returned to our lives. And it was so within oneself as well. For so many of us, we could say *I* and it was not a lie. And when *I* appear, time returns to one's life.

The "earthquake" of September 11 brought some of this element, but its main characteristic was quite different. People also acted as though they were brought in front of some great truth, but instead of the shock of finding out who we really were as human beings, instead of approaching the remembering of our Selves, September 11 brought us something different, but deeply complementary. Instead of the gift of presence, instead of the *response* of *I am*, it brought the equally real *question: Who am I?*—as an American, yes, but, more importantly, as a human being. Are we (am I) living in a fantasy, a dream? Is it true that they, whoever *they* are, want to kill *me*? This was not nature speaking, not cosmic law, not the intrinsic mortality of man, awareness of which releases the Self from its covering. This was man speaking with all his fear and hatred, his bewilderment in front of his own manifestations and the manifestations of his neighbor. The fragility of everything we are accustomed to was exposed in both "earthquakes"—but the 1989 earthquake revealed at the same time the greatness and the force of universal nature—and with it the hint of the eternal within oneself.

The "earthquake" of September 11 exposed the fragility of our world and at the same time revealed how far we are from the eternal within ourselves! It was exactly the opposite truth—yet joined at its ends, like the mythic ouroboros serpent that swallows its own tail. The literal earthquake woke us up to the Self; September 11 woke us up to the ego, the false self, the root of all the evil that enters the earth and destroys human life, and with it, of course, the reality of time, the reality of lived presence. The ego lives only in the future and the past; it has no present moment; it is always hurrying or dreaming.

But—and here the two shocks meet—in seeing the ego, in seeing the fear and violence and unreality of our lives, the real Self appears as a call. And here, too, the problem and mystery of time come together in the great question of the sense and purpose of our lived life. The shock of seeing and feeling the reality of man's fallen self sounds as a call not only for America, but for oneself. This call is easily expressed in words, and up to a point easily understood, though of immense difficulty to obey: *You must change your life!*

And with this call time returns to our world. Another intention returns to our day-to-day existence as individuals and as a society. We must seek for conscience within ourselves and with our neighbors. We must work to become real, to exist fully, to be able to give and to help. All the values that we hold dear as America, or as Christians or Jews or Moslems or as humanists, as independent thinkers, as scientists seeking the mind of nature

in the facts of nature—whoever we are, we hold fundamental values which in order to be lived require that we
come into being, into real existence within ourselves. *We
must seek to become the people we are searching for.* And then
we can even be very, very busy; we can even have full calendars and e-mail and computers doing everything too
fast. We can even be doing things right away. But it will
be as though it is all repeating itself in another dimension
of time—with oneself as the timeless witness consciously
living the life we have been given. Within it all we will be
searching for our Selves. And to search for one's Self is
already to exist *now.*

Such was and is the message of this book: *When the
people return to the earth, then time will return to the earth.*

PROLOGUE

This book is addressed to everyone who is starved for time. That is, it is addressed to everyone. We are all living in a culture that traps us into doing too many things, taking on too many responsibilities, facing too many choices and saying yes to too many opportunities. Nearing the end of over a century of inventions designed to save time, we find ourselves bereft of time itself. As Jeremy Rifkin has pointed out, "we have surrounded ourselves with time-saving technological gadgetry, only to be overwhelmed by plans that cannot be carried out, appointments that cannot be honored, schedules that cannot be fulfilled, and deadlines that cannot be met."[1] It is the new poverty, the poverty of our affluence. It is our famine, the famine of a culture that has chosen things over time, the external world over the inner world.

It has become the aching question of our era. What used to be considered a sign of success—being busy,

having many responsibilities, being involved in many
projects or activities—is not being felt as an affliction. It
is leading us nowhere. More and more it is being experienced as meaningless.

This is the real significance of our problem with time.
It is a crisis of meaning. What has disappeared is meaningful time. It is not technology or the accelerating influence of money; it is not global capitalism that is responsible for the time famine. The root of our modern
problem with time is neither technological, sociological,
economic nor psychological. It is metaphysical. It is a
question of the meaning of human life itself. The aim of
this book is to uncover the link between our pathology of
time and the eternal mystery of what a human being is
meant to be in the universal scheme of things. The wisdom teachings of the world, each in its own way, have
spoken of what we may call the soul, the spirit, the timeless, the eternal in man. But the challenge is to approach
these ancient ideas in a way that is practical, that can
actually lead us toward a solution of our problem. Words
alone, no matter how sacred; ideas alone, no matter how
profound, are not enough to help us confront our problem with time. But words, properly received; ideas,
thoughtfully pondered; stories and images heard and
attended to with an open heart, can help us feel the relationship between the question of our being and the problem of our life in time, after which ideas can find their
proper place in our minds. In any case, this is how I have
written this book. A story and an image can enter our

psyche in a way that concepts and analyses cannot. And so this examination of time and the human soul should perhaps begin, as all true stories begin, with the suddenly pregnant phrase:

"Once upon a time . . ."

PART I

ONCE
UPON
A TIME

CHAPTER 1

THE MAN WITH THE SOFT BROWN EYES

There is a novel I want to write. The hero is a man of fifty, which was my age when I began dreaming of this story. His life is in crisis, as was my own then, and through magic he is sent back in time to meet himself at the age of sixteen. The hero's name is Eliot: Eliot Appleman. My name is Jacob: Jacob Needleman.

I speak of this as a fiction, but in my heart I don't think of it that way. Doesn't the sixteen-year-old Jacob (or Jerry, as I am called) still exist? And isn't it possible to go back and be with him? Time? Surely, time is not what we think it is. We are wrong about so many lesser things; how could we imagine we understand the greatest of all mysteries, time?

The hero of my story, Eliot Appleman, is a psychiatrist. As for myself, I am a professor of philosophy. Both Eliot and I presume to an ability to see beneath the surface of human affairs. He has been trained to look into the psyche for hidden patterns and I, the philosopher, regard the whole world as a tissue of appearances, behind which there operate great laws that can be discerned only through what the ancient teachers called wisdom.

In the course of this story the older Eliot learns that he cannot navigate his life without opening his mind and heart to a reality that the scientifically trained "Dr. Appleman" might have regarded as a mystical fantasy. Here, too, my own life corresponds, but in a reverse way: in that critical period of my life I was to learn that one cannot go far with great metaphysical questions, such as the question of time, without the hard work of confronting one's own inner emptiness.

PHILADELPHIA: 1952

I dream most often of the novel's opening scenes in which the two Eliots first meet each other. The teenage Eliot is at a restaurant in downtown Philadelphia with a young woman who is a year older. Her name is Elaine. He is falling in love for the first time in his life.

It is Saturday afternoon, the last weekend of the summer. The Turin Grotto is busy; black-jacketed waiters are everywhere on the run. The older Eliot quietly arranges to be seated at a table next to the two young people. They are absorbed in each other and do not notice him. Breathlessly, he eavesdrops on their conversation and watches them out of the corner of his eye.

The teacher who sent Eliot back in time gave him no special instructions about the laws of time travel. And Eliot was so stunned by what was being offered him that he did not even ask questions.

He has been sent back to study himself at what seemed to him to be a decisive and defining moment in his life. Nothing is said to him about whether he is allowed to intervene in the past and influence the future. Eliot soon discovers why such a warning has not been given: it is simply not necessary. The events of our lives are so tightly interconnected, and our lives as a whole proceed within such a vast network of purposes which we do not see, that no ordinary man or woman is able to know the real turning points of his or her life, the real crossroads where meaningful change can take place. Without that kind of knowledge, we can press and poke at our lives where we will, but it will have no more effect than a temporary disturbance that soon closes over again, as tissue closes over a minor wound. The kind of changes we seek to make in our lives are usually no more than superficial wounds in the body of time.

What Eliot is overhearing at the table next to him is a tumultuous conversation during which the young woman begins to cry. As yet, the older Eliot is so overwhelmed by the mere fact of his being there that he cannot even trust himself to look at the young Eliot. I mean to make a great deal of the moment when the two Eliots first look into each other's eyes. The younger Eliot will instinctively turn away without knowing why—as though he had just touched fire. The older Eliot will feel a tender sadness and the hint of a kind of love for which he has no name. I want to treat that moment as an example of what happens inside all of us when we even fleetingly breach our ordinary sense of time. What we loosely call memory is, in fact, the surface of a capacity that, in its depths, offers the only hope for mankind and for us as individuals. But we are content and conditioned to stay on the surface of memory; and there, on the surface of memory, we remain prisoners of time.

The older Eliot struggles to find an attitude of objectivity as he hears the young woman's tearful accusations. He knows very well the effect they will have on the young Eliot and what that portends about his whole future. But it is not the kind of knowing that makes a difference.

The older Eliot believed that he remembered this particular scene. But he sees now that he did not remember it at all. So that is what she really said! So that is how she really acted! No wonder I was so helpless!

Suddenly, she puts a cigarette between her lips. The young Eliot fumbles, looking everywhere for a match. Without thinking twice, the older man reaches over with his lighter. The woman looks at him with dark eyes as she lights her cigarette. A powerful current flows between them. His hand grazes hers as he takes the lighter away.

TIME AND PASSION

The older man's heart pounds and he hastily turns back to his table as an anguished passion begins to rise in him. Emotions that are part of our essence do not change. They are covered over, but great feeling is not in time. It is always now; it does not know about the future or the past.

Very well, then, with what do we perceive the passage of time? Is time only a construction of thought—thought disconnected from feeling? Yet nothing seems more real and unchangeable than time and its passing. Nothing seems more constricting than the limitations of time. And nothing more powerful than our impulse to live, to live longer, to live forever and not disappear in the unholy infinity of unending time. Do we have so little time in our lives because we allow ourselves so little real passion?

The young woman runs out of the restaurant and the young Eliot remains at the table, sunk in confusion and despair. The older man hesitatingly starts to go over to him, but the young Eliot suddenly throws money on the table and runs out after the woman. The older man remains at his table and tries calmly to drink his cold water and to remember the aim for which he came back in time: to study, to understand.

TO EVERY THING THERE IS A SEASON

It has long ago been said that time does not exist in itself. What we call time is an abstraction, something for

philosophers to analyze and for scientists to make use of
in their equations. Time in itself cannot be seen or sensed.
Yet it enters into everything, as was said by Solomon the
Preacher. Everything, everything has its own kind of
time. And we will never solve the problem of time without understanding this ancient truth. We will never
"manage" time, we will never understand our past, we will
never be able to prepare our future without grasping the
unique coloration of time in every real, human event, or
every real, cosmic event—which means events that have
breadth, length, love and hate, light and fury, energy,
meaning, struggle and the silence of universal law. This
universe, this galaxy, this earth, this body we call our own,
all live and breathe and feel and have mind—and therefore they are infused by time. It is not only we who love
and hate, who sow and reap. It is true of everything each
in its way. What the Preacher has said of human life is
actually being said of all that exists under the hand of
God—that is, "under the sun."

> To every thing there is a season, and a time to
>   every purpose under the heaven;
> A time to be born, and a time to die; a time to plant,
>   and a time to pluck up that which is planted;
> A time to kill, and a time to heal; a time to
>   break down, and a time to build up;
> A time to weep, and a time to laugh; a time to
>   mourn, and a time to dance . . .[2]

THE LIE OF MEMORY

The scene shifts to later in the day. The older Eliot is driving in a car. He knows—he remembers—where to find the younger Eliot.

The young Eliot is on his way home, slowly walking along a parkway in the oppressive afternoon heat, not really caring what happens. The older Eliot slows the car as he approaches his younger self dejectedly walking along the edge of the parkway. For a brief moment he thinks of what he has left in order to come back in time. Back there, everywhere he turned he was crashing against the lies that made up his life. The facade of a "shared understanding" with his wife could no longer conceal the lack of any real connection between them. The young heart within him long ago was left to live on fantasy and resignation. As for his children, his natural love for them was again and again thwarted by ideas of what a father was supposed to be and by preconceived ideas of how his children were supposed to be toward him: lies in the form of guilt alternating with resentment. His profession? How long had it been since the trained psychiatrist had actually heard or *seen* a patient? Lies in the form of techniques that masqueraded as attention. What had become of the yearning for truth that had first drawn him to his work, where was the love of reality that saw the laws of God in the laws of the mind? Was that young physician still alive—somewhere in him, somewhere in time?

With sudden, startling clarity he sees the self-pitying slope of young Eliot's shoulders, a vision that goes straight into the older man's heart and soul and makes him aware of the essence of this characteristic emotion of his. This one glimpse shows the trained psychiatrist that neither his nor his patients' memories are as real or as deep as they need to be. My God, he thinks as he slows the car beside the boy, I have never *really* remembered; no one has. What a fraud: all this remembering is only the work of a small part of the mind, mixing its accidental thoughts and feelings with scattered, random fragments of the past. We have never deeply remembered! We have never really gone back in time. We have never seen the roots of our being with the whole of our mind.

FATE AND THE REAL FUTURE

Walking along the edge of the parkway, the young man is now aware of the dark green car slowing down alongside him. The passenger door opens.

"Need a lift?" the driver says.

Eliot had never before hitchhiked or accepted a ride from a stranger. But now, without the slightest hesitation, he jumps into the car and shuts the door. For a moment he wonders at that. Perhaps, he thinks, he was so preoccupied with his worries that he had no room in his mind to be afraid or even normally cautious. Or perhaps it was something else.

The car speeds off. "Where are you going?" the stranger asks.

How will this scene now proceed? How to understand what happens in us when we first make contact with our fate? Fate: the word has lost its meaning for us, it has become a cliché; at best a superstition. But suppose there really exists such a thing as fate? Suppose, underneath the windswept ripples of our everyday battles with time, our anxious, everyday efforts to steer our lives, there exists a deeper current carrying something essential in us to a predetermined future? And what would that something be within ourselves that lives, or tries to live, wants to live, beneath the surface of time as we know it; that wants to break into the daylight of our consciousness—there to grow with us, perhaps? What happens in an individual when we first feel that something deeper within ourselves is calling to us, trying to see us, not only from the past but from the future—a future we cannot even imagine in the midst of our crowded, complicated minutes, hours and days, but which is in fact what we are really starving for when we are starved for time?

To the question, "Where are you going?" the young Eliot is tempted to answer, "Anywhere, I don't care." But instead he says, simply:

"Home."

Eliot is only vaguely aware that stranger seems to know which route to take. He is drowning in his emotions about Elaine. Why was she trying to push him away, and why did her pushing him away have the effect of making him even more attached to her? More willing to make insane promises to her that would destroy his life?

The car is humming along the leafy East River Parkway, heading toward North Philadelphia. The open windows let in the hot, humid wind carrying the fragrances of late August.

The voice of the stranger breaks into young Eliot's thoughts:

"I guess pretty soon school will be starting for you."

Eliot turns his head to look at him: stocky, medium height with broad shoulders; small, sinewy hands gripping the wheel. His longish hair and wispy beard are faded brown heavily streaked with gray. Young Eliot rightly guesses him to be about fifty.

Eliot feels a sensation of warmth and relaxation and starts to respond to the small-talk question about school. But thoughts of Elaine are commanding his attention. Of course, he cannot know that his actual future is sitting there next to him, plainly visible, and that the relaxation he feels is, in part, due to his subliminal intuition that nothing of what he fears is going to happen. He cannot consciously know that his fear and anguish about the future are based completely on imagination—or, rather, one part truth to a hundred parts imagination. He cannot know this, but still he is bemused to see how easily he is set free for a moment from his anguish. Nevertheless, he turns his attention back to Elaine—in a sense, he *allows* his attention to be swallowed up again by fear and imagination.

My intention here is to let the story begin to explore our general pathology of time—in this case our crippled relationship to the future. Under the surface of our continual worrying, our tense efforts to foresee and manipulate the future in our thoughts and in the countless unnecessary actions that are, simply, what we may rightly call a *waste of time*—under the surface of all this agitation, which comprises so much of our waking life, there is a knowing which can be very deeply hidden, but which sometimes surfaces for a moment—as in the ancient symbol of a great, wise fish brooding deep beneath the surface of the waters. In certain symbologies this profound inner knowing is represented by the salmon—which takes its name from Solomon the Wise. Not only is this the wisest of the creatures of the deep, but its action is directed toward one thing—to struggle with incomprehensible perseverance against the onrushing current. There is a wisdom in us that knows and intends in a manner that we are blind to while in the course of our lives we are driven helplessly away from our source by the currents of automatic time. There is that in us which could give us an entirely different kind of future than the one we are trying to fabricate in our anxious imaginings, and an entirely different kind of future than what actually awaits us at the end of our individual allotment of automatically flowing time. But, as we are, we do not and cannot see the future for what it is. All our agitation, all our planning and preparing, all our manipulations never lead us toward the future as it actually takes form. We can barely even imagine what it will be like to cross to the other side of the room, far less imagine what our life will actually be like in five years or one or six months or even in a week or a day. It is one of the fundamental illusions of humankind that we can imagine the future in any true sense. We may pick certain aspects of the future and predict them, but the main thrust of the future, with all its levels of interconnecting events and detail, is never seen at all. This lack is due to our state of being; it has nothing whatever to do with the nature of time itself.

THE FIRST LOOK

Eliot keeps casting sidelong glances at the stranger, who has kept his eyes forward and has allowed the silence to exist without attempting further conversation. But when the car leaves the parkway and is stopped at a traffic light, the stranger suddenly turns to face Eliot.

"Where do you want to go?"

Eliot now finds himself looking at the stranger full face. He opens his mouth to answer him, but no words can come out. Instead, he sharply turns his head away. Suddenly his breathing is coming hard. Why? There is nothing at all sinister in the man's face, quite the contrary. The soft brown eyes, flecked with green and yellow, are warm and radiant. The well-formed features could be those of a child except that they are packed together with such intensity. The smile is full of light, although the forehead is deeply creased by the tracks of concerns that never let go.

Eliot cautiously turns his head to look once more at the stranger, who is now concentrating again on the road. He stares at the profile, transfixed. His breathing is still labored and his heart is pounding. On the stranger's temple, partially concealed by unruly tufts of gray-brown hair, Eliot discerns the horizontal indentation of a wing-shaped scar. With trembling fingers, he reaches up to the right side of his own face, afraid of what he will find, yet knowing full well that the same scar, with precisely the same strange winglike form marks his own skin!

He violently jerks his hand away from his own scar and swivels his head forward, staring through the windshield at the oncoming cars. He is shivering and his breathing now comes in throaty staccato bursts.

"Don't be frightened," says the stranger, easing the car through heavy traffic of the afternoon rush hour. His soothing words have little effect. For a fleeting moment Eliot has the impulse to open the door and leap out. But of course he doesn't. In the first place, he would probably get killed, and in the second place, he is so frozen with fear that he can't move a muscle anywhere in his body. And in the third place, he reasons, this is probably a dream anyway. He is probably at home on the living-room couch dozing, as he sometimes does, with his head bent sideways at a crazy angle.

But he knows very well that he is not dreaming.

"Don't be frightened," the stranger repeats. And, in fact, alongside the sense of terror, Eliot again detects the stirring of something warm and pleasant, this time in his chest. But when he moves his eyes and looks again at the stranger, he is once more engulfed by fear.

We often say we wish to see into the future. But to see into the future would mean to see into ourselves, to see what our choices really have been and to see the consequences of all our actions. But it would also mean—and here terror enters—seeing how little we have understood what life is really for; it would mean seeing what we have thrown away. It is only children or fools—so wisdom teaches—who imagine that the passage of time obeys the trivial laws and patterns that we live by from minute to minute and hour to hour as we nervously consult our watches and our calendars. Only fools—fools like us—think we can "manage" the great river of time. Time flows through us and is spent in our thoughts and feelings and sensations—not only in the external activities of our lives, our dealings, our triumphs and defeats. Only fools imagine they can manage time without mastering the constant inner flow of thought, emotion and sensation. When Reality comes toward us—not the little facts we earnestly call by that name, but the timeless objective truth about what man is and is meant to be—we automatically run from it and what it shows us of our ego's insignificance. Yet also underneath the surface of our socially constructed persona, our ego, there is that same calm knowing, like a warmth, an intimation of joy. Young Eliot feels terror, the terror of being visited by a force infinitely beyond his comprehension; the terror of being seen by his own eyes! How can the greatness of Reality, a greatness that encompasses all the worlds above and below—how can that infinite greatness have my own face, my own eyes? The ancient Hindu teaching that ultimate reality is the consciousness of *I*—is that actually more than just an interesting, or perhaps inspiring, metaphysical concept? Is it really concretely true, true of *me*?

Why are we afraid of being seen—by ourselves?

There exists an entirely different kind of fear than the fear our upbringing and psychological world have injected into us: a fear of objective truth. The "person" Eliot Appleman, the young man seated next to the driver and the one hidden inside the driver himself, that "person" has been fabricated by the world in order to ward off truth! That "person" in ourselves is formed to protect us from the contradictory messages coming to us from the so-called "real" world. Why has this deformation occurred? Because, so wisdom teaches, society long ago ceased to send us messages of objective truth that call us to struggle for individual being. The "world" does not know about the cosmos and its laws full of purpose and conscious order. The message of the cosmos to man—as we hear from the ancient teachings—is: although you are mortal, although your time is finite, you have within you that which can transcend time. Freedom from time—the approximate term for which is "immortality"—awaits you; you are made for that, but you must search and search to receive in your life the winds of this immortality, this endless presence, that are constantly being sent to man from the center of the universe.

TIME AND FEAR

Our world, our culture, is not the cosmos and it sends a different kind of message to us: your time is finite and you are finite. Whether the message has God in it or speaks against God does not matter; behind it is the same terrifying vision that compels the personality of a man or woman to develop around a lie. The world is lying to us about the cosmos; the world is lying to us about reality. At the very beginning of our lives it tells us the universe is going to hurt us, destroy us. It tells us these things not necessarily through concepts and ideas, but through the anxious behavior and the deep-down faithlessness of our elders. God or no God, it rarely makes a difference. The personality is formed to protect us from metaphysical pain. And it does this very well. Too well. Woe to him who cannot tell the difference between the fear of objective truth—a truth which exposes us to our lies in order to show us the fundamental love at the heart of reality—and the fear of the false universe which our world injects into us.

In the false world, time is our enemy, but we do not really know how powerful it is; we don't really *feel* the deep, rolling, cruel power of the river of time, so busy are we managing the crisscrossing waves on the surface. But in the real world there is a wind that comes from "the center of the universe," from the "beginning"—in the language of myth. "Long ago," "once upon a time," a message and a messenger were sent to humankind. This messenger is always being sent.

I want this scene in the novel to evoke the feeling of the first actual contact that a man or woman can have with this other message and this other fear, this good fear that threatens everything in us which has conformed itself to the lie. This good fear is sometimes known to us as the experience of the *uncanny*. Experiences that break through our ordinary sense of time often have this element of the uncanny about them.

WHO ARE YOU?

For the first time in my life, I *am seen*. And what is it that sees me? I am seen by something in myself that is outside of time, something that is always there, calling to me. What is it? Who . . . ?

Eliot closes his eyes and tries again and again to fight down the terror that is causing him to tremble all over his body. Through clenched teeth he slowly, agonizingly, pushes out the words, "Who are you?"

The stranger waits a moment, then answers, softly, calmly:

"Who do you think I am?"

The young Eliot keeps his eyes closed and says nothing. He senses the car turning, slowing to a stop, backing up, parking. He does not want to say who he thinks the stranger is. He doesn't even want to think it.

With his eyes still closed, he says only:

"What do you want with me?" His heart is now pounding so strongly it seems it will burst.

The stranger answers in a whisper.

"Nothing, Eliot. I don't want anything from you. Please don't be frightened of me." The car stops and the motor is turned off.

Eliot is not surprised that the stranger knows his name, and the sound of his voice is so pleasant that Eliot is ready to look at him again.

He turns his head toward him.

He opens his eyes.

He cannot bear it for more than a second. The stranger's soft brown eyes simply look at him with full attention. They make no demand upon him, yet they stay gently and completely upon him. They do not bore into him, they do not waver, yet they are not ferociously steady. They do not drill into him. They do not judge him. They do not desire him. They are not distracted. They simply look at him with a calm light. For Eliot, it is like touching fire; it is unbearable.

He closes his eyes and begins to sob. Slowly, he pushes down the door handle and opens the door of his car. He sticks his leg out of the car, as though to leave, still quietly sobbing. But he does not leave.

He is not aware that the stranger himself has closed his eyes; that he himself cannot hold that look so free of judging and partiality. The older Eliot is also trembling.

When *seeing* enters one's life a new kind of fear enters with it. And a new question about time, a completely new question.

CHAPTER 2

TIME: A NEW QUESTION

D o we have the courage to approach the question of time from the depths of our heart? Before we try to face the question of time as a *problem*, the problem of how to manage our lives, can we stay with it long enough to hear it calling to us purely and simply as a *question*, the question of who we are and why we are alive at all? It takes courage to stay with it as a question when all around us, with ever more insistence, our culture treats it as a problem, and makes it into a problem. A problem is something we are supposed to deal with; a problem demands that we do something, change something. A problem is something we are suppose to solve.

But time is more than a problem; it is a question, perhaps the greatest question that a man or woman can face and perhaps the most important one. Such great questions cannot be answered with the part of the mind that solves problems. They need to be deeply felt and experienced long, long before they can begin to be answered. We need to *feel* the question of time much more deeply and simply than we do. We agitate about the problem of time, but we seldom *feel* what it means.

Somewhere in my novel I want to have the older Eliot meeting his mother and father. At that moment in time Eliot's parents are younger than he is. I want the scene to have the young Eliot in it as well. The young Eliot has to some extent come to accept the identity of the stranger, but he is very afraid of what will happen when his mother and father meet him. He is afraid of what the shock will do to them. The stranger tries to reassure him, but to no avail.

The scene is set at a parent-faculty meeting in the school gymnasium. After introducing the older man as one of the school's counselors, Eliot looks on unbelievingly at what takes place. Neither his mother nor his father shows any sign at all of recognizing the stranger! There is not the slightest hint that they see anything unusual! Not the slightest discomfort; their awkwardness is no more than they always manifest with strangers. Eliot is both relieved and disappointed and he doesn't know why. He hears himself saying to himself, almost in an audible whisper: "Look, Mom! Look, closely!" Inexplicably, he is much more relieved that his father is unaware of the stranger's identity.

THE REAL PAST

But the older Eliot is profoundly shaken. His legs are quivering as he looks into the eyes of his mother and as he grasps the strong, dry hand of his father. He is stunned by his impulse to grab his father and embrace him.

The past: you cannot go there so simply, so cleanly. Do not imagine that you can. The emotions you will feel— yes, we know about some of them from the psychotherapists and the psychiatrists: guilt, for example, or resentment, or self-pity. "Dr. Appleman" has seen these emotions in a thousand patients. But they are not the feelings through which a man or woman may meet the past. These emotions of everyday life or the emotions that appear in the therapist's office, or over a bottle of wine, or at three in the morning—they are not the antennae that connect us to our real past. *These emotions arise to protect us from the past, not to reveal it.* They live in the intermediate world, between the mechanisms of the ego and the infinitely subtle power of the heart that was known to the ancient masters under the name of *conscience*. It is conscience that lives in the deep unconscious of man, and do not imagine you can easily bear to have it awakened in you. This conscience comes from God, not from anything that is socially conditioned.

The past and the future: conscience and will. We know nothing of these things that are of the true nature of man, that are calling to us from our inner world.

"Pleased to meet you, Mr. . . ." Eliot's mother politely waits to be told his name. Neither the older nor the younger Eliot had foreseen the need for a name. The older Eliot is dumbfounded. He tries to collect himself enough to grab at the first name that comes—anything at all will do. But, shocked and amazed, he hears himself saying to his mother, "I'm Eliot, I'm Eliot!"

The older man feels the horrified stare of the younger upon him. At the same time, an impulse to laugh begins to rise up in him. He tries to think of something clever to say to ease the situation, but before he can open his mouth again his mother is replying with a kindly smile, "I'm very pleased to meet you, Mr. Ellison. Eliot has told us a great deal about you."

Of course. The teacher who sent him back told him this would happen. People cannot perceive what they cannot believe. I hear the teacher preparing Eliot for his journey back in time and telling him something like this:

"There are many who have taken this journey; you are not the first. There are many beings around us and many things happen right before our eyes that would answer all our deepest questions if we could only see them for what they are. We do not live in the real world. Don't be afraid; no one else will discover who you are. Don't waste your energy hiding. On the contrary, try to become known to your young self. Try to make him trust you. Everything depends on that. In the beginning, his reactions will pass back and forth from disbelief to fear and then to interest. Bur not until he begins to trust you, to trust you when you are in his presence, will you begin to understand what you need to understand."

The older Eliot had thought he was going back in time only in order to see, to study—as he had come to understand these words. But very soon he begins to realize that he cannot really see his younger self without the arising of a certain love, a certain yearning and a certain trust.

How insane to believe we can grasp anything essential about time without opening the heart. There is nothing about time we can perceive or hold on to without the maturation of our conscious feelings. The god of time laughs at our little watches and calendars. Like God Himself, time punishes us by simply leaving us to our own devices. What could be more painful than to try to manipulate the greatest force in the universe—time— with our nervous minds, our anxious hearts, our tortured bodies? Until we can let in what the masters of wisdom called "the attention that comes from the source," the wind that rises from the center of the world, or simply "divine love," we can no more "deal" with time than we can "deal" with volcanoes or earthquakes or the movement of the earth around the sun.

The older Eliot slowly regains his composure. Mercifully, the vision of all that he has done and not done for his mother and father recedes back to the bottom of the ocean where conscience dwells. His mind slowly becomes bright and alert, but his mask begins to crack again when his mother goes on.

"Eliot has spoken very highly of you, Mr. Ellison."

This is a lie. Why is his mother lying? The older Eliot is aware that his father is standing rock still. Is he staring at him? Does he suspect something?

The older Eliot's knees tremble again as his mother, sipping charmingly at her cup of punch and smiling with that sweetly feminine light in her eyes, says, "What do you think of our Eliot?" She puts her arm around the young man's shoulder.

The older man cannot speak. He is choked with emotion. He looks to his father, who is still standing helplessly to the side. There is a drama being played out here, Dr. Appleman knows that. A man or a woman spends his or her whole life playing and replaying one scene—with his mother or father. And time moves us on between the enactment and the reenactment of this scene, this scene which never moves, never changes, is never done with. The older Eliot could feel the touch of his mother's hand on this shoulder.

THE TIME OF THE HEART

He thinks to himself: Will I die someday without ever having played through this scene and freed myself from it? I know she will die and I know when. It will be thirty years from now. But the scene will keep on playing again and again. I will grow old, my hair will turn white, my shoulders will stoop with age and my eyes grow dim and this scene will play on and on, over and over again. There is a kind of time that takes place outside of this scene. A nonpsychological time, the time of inanimate nature, the time of machines. But the time of the heart is separated from that. The time of the heart does not move, it repeats over and over again in cycles, like a cry or a laugh echoing in the endless night or endless day.

We have cut off the time of the heart from the time of the physical world. It is an artificial separation. When ancient peoples—cultures still informed by the old wisdom—spoke of time as a cycle, it was because the drama of the heart and the life of nature and matter were not isolated from each other. Science gave us our mastery over nature by cutting away the time of the heart. We live in inorganic time. We can no more master inorganic time than we can walk through solid matter. Our flesh cannot penetrate this kind of time. Time as we know it is no more or less than solid matter extended and attenuated.

This is the new question: what do we need from our feelings in order to overcome the intractability of time? When modern man began to conquer matter through the development of science and technology, he didn't see the point when he began to be conquered *by* matter. The point when he—where *we* became like inorganic matter ourselves in our feeling, where our hearts became logical and the meanings in our lives became calculable, numerable, quantifiable, measured by money.

A tranquil heart is never defeated by time. Under the surface of our obsessed emotional reactions, deeply hidden, is a source of feeling that constantly pours itself out, circulating through the whole of our being, down to the cells and tissues of our mortal body. The wisdom literature of the Judaic tradition named this function *da'at*, the "heart of the world," the heart of the little world that is man. It is a subtle life that moves through all the worlds of creation and life, binding together and nourishing both the rigorous world of logic and law and the merciful world of inclusion and forgiveness.

To forgive is *to start again*. To judge is *to be brought to an end*. The vision of the ancient wisdom brings both forgiveness and judgment into relationship. There is the time of forgiveness and the time of judgment. Together, they both exist in the law of *cycles*. We are judged and forgiven at the same moment through the existence of cycles and repetition. The sorrow of our modern life is that we live in one part of time—the time of judgment, where things end, where everything flows toward death. Such is the life we have invented in our little boat whose engine is helpless against the immense tide of automatic time. And there we live entirely unaware that we need only raise our sail and be moved by "the wind that comes from the center of the world." The ancient wisdom looks at us and sees a civilization imagining that time is linear while this same civilization turns round and round in the greater cycles of birth, death, and rebirth.

CHAPTER 3

TIME: PROBLEM, QUESTION AND MYSTERY

If we listen to the teachings of the ancient wisdom, we will hear them telling us that none of our methods for mastering time can work. The reason they cannot work is that we do not *feel* that we exist, we do not see ourselves with the soft eyes of the heart. One of the central texts of the Buddhist tradition tells us, from the very first sentence:

> *We are what we think.*
> *All that we are arises with our thoughts.*
> *With our thoughts we make the world.*[3]

And having told us this, the text goes on to show us the need to come to an entirely new kind of *feeling* about ourselves and a new way of seeing ourselves that is informed by this feeling. We need to *feel* our mortality, and not just know it with our thought. What the ancient teachings mean by *mind* is not what we mean by the word. When they speak of mind they are speaking of a capacity of understanding that blends intellect and heart and instinct. What is the point, they tell us, of managing our day more efficiently if we don't understand what our days are for, where they are meant to lead us? But when we begin to feel the importance of the question of why we exist at all, our obsessions begin to weaken their hold. When obsessiveness recedes, even if only slightly, a crowded day contains more time. But we cannot use tricks and techniques that serve only to make our obsessiveness more "efficient." There are no tricks or techniques that can make us feel that we exist. And it is only at such levels of feeling—and far beyond such levels—that time begins to "breathe" in our life. Only with such feeling do *we* begin to breathe differently, literally and figuratively. According to the ancient wisdom, when a human being breathes differently the passage of time takes on new properties. There is a new feeling of self that appears when a man or woman truly and genuinely steps back from himself, looks at himself and then . . . ? And then: *enters himself.*

How to understand this mystery? We turn again to the language of story and image.

THE STORY OF KIRZAI

Not long after I began dreaming of my novel I encountered a tale purportedly from Central Asia. I never learned, and was never able to verify, where this tale actually originated. In all my studies of the myths and fables of other cultures I had never encountered anything exactly like it. And the fact that it came to my attention just after I had conceived the idea of the two Eliots made me feel that I was suddenly living within the very kind of mystery and magic I wanted to write about. Here is the tale:

Long ago there was a young merchant named Kirzai whose business called him one day to travel to the village of Tchigan two hundred kilometers away. Ordinarily, he would have taken the route that followed along the edge of the mountains, enabling him to make most of his journey protected from the sun. But on this occasion Kirzai was under the pressure of time; it was urgent that he get to Tchigan as soon as possible. And so he decided to strike out directly across the Syr Darya desert.

The Syr Darya desert is known for the intensity of its sun and very few dare to venture across it. Nevertheless, Kirzai watered his camel, filled his gourds and set off on his journey.

Several hours after he left, the desert wind began to rise. Kirzai grumbled to himself and quickened the pace of his camel. Suddenly he stopped, stupefied. About a hundred meters ahead of him there rose up a gigantic whirlwind. Never had Kirzai seen anything like it. It cast a strange purple light all around it; even the color of the sand was changed.

Kirzai hesitated. Should he make a lengthy detour in order to avoid this strange apparition or should he continue straight ahead? Kirzai was in a great hurry; he felt he did not have the time to take the slower path, so he lowered his head, hunched his shoulders and advanced forward.

To his surprise, the moment he entered the storm everything became much calmer. The wind no longer cut so sharply against his face. He felt pleased that he had made the right decision.

But suddenly he was compelled to stop again. A few steps ahead a man lay stretched upon the ground next to a crouching camel. Kirzai immediately dismounted to see what was wrong.

The man's head was wrapped in a scarf, but Kirzai could tell that he was old.

The old man opened his eyes, looked at Kirzai intently for a moment and then said in a hoarse whisper:

"Is it . . . you?"

Kirzai laughed and shook his head.

"What? Don't tell me you know who I am! Has my fame spread to the desert of Syr Darya? But you, old man, who are you?"

The man said nothing. Kirzai continued:

"In any case, you are not well. Where are you going?"

"To Givah," the old man sighed. "But I have no more water."

Kirzai reflected. He could certainly share some of his water with the old man, but if he did he risked running out of water himself.

But he could not just leave him. A man is not a dog to be left dying without a backward glance.

To the devil with my plans, Kirzai thought. I need only find my way to the path along the mountains if I need more water. A human life counts more than a business appointment!

He helped the old man drink some water, filled one of his gourds and then helped him mount his camel.

"Go straight ahead that way," he said, pointing his finger, "and you'll be in Givah within two hours."

The old man made a sign of acknowledgment with his hands. Before leaving, he looked for a long moment at Kirzai and uttered these strange words:

"One day the desert will repay you."

He then spurred his camel in the direction that Kirzai had indicated. Kirzai continued his journey. The opportunity that had been waiting for him in Tchigan was no doubt lost, but he felt at peace with himself.

Time passed. Thirty years later Kirzai's business took him continually back and forth between Givah and Tchigan. He had not become rich, but what he earned was enough to provide a good life for his family. He did not ask for more than that.

One day, when he was selling hides at the marketplace in Tchigan, he learned that his son was gravely ill. It was urgent that he go to him immediately. Kirzai did not

hesitate. He remembered the shortcut across the desert
that he had wanted to take thirty years before. He
watered his camel, filled his gourds and set off.

Along the way he battled against time, spurring his
camel unceasingly. He did not stop or even slow down
while drinking, and because of that the accident occurred.
His gourd suddenly fell from his hands, and before he was
able to get down to retrieve it the water disappeared into
the sand. Kirzai cursed out loud. With only one full gourd
it was impossible to cross the dessert. But, thinking of his
son, the old man pushed himself onward:

"I must do it, I *will* do it!"

The sun of the Syr Darya desert is merciless. It cares
little why or for what purpose a man tries to brave its rays;
it blazed unremittingly with always the same power and
intensity. Kirzai soon realized that he had made a great
mistake. His tongue became parched; his skin burned.
His only remaining gourd was already empty. And now,
to his dismay, he saw that a sandstorm was beginning.
Kirzai wrapped his head in his scarf, closed his eyes and
let his camel carry him forward where it would. He was
no longer conscious of anything.

A gigantic whirlwind now rose up in front of him. It
gave off a soft purple light, but Kirzai remained nearly
unconscious and saw nothing. His camel entered into the
whirlwind, advanced a few steps and then abruptly sat
down. Kirzai tumbled onto the ground.

I'm finished, he thought. My son will never see me
again!

All at once, however, he gave a cry of joy. A man mounted on a camel was moving toward him. But the closer the man came, the more Kirzai's joy turned into stupefaction.

This man who was now dismounting from his camel—Kirzai knew him! He recognized his youthful face, his clothes—even the camel that he was riding! A camel that Kirzai himself had bought for two valuable vases many years before.

Kirzai was certain: the young man who had come to help him was himself! It was Kirzai himself as he was thirty years before!

"Is it . . . you?" said Kirzai in a hoarse whisper.

The young man looked at him and laughed.

"What? Don't tell me you know who I am! Has my fame spread to the desert of Syr Darya? But you, old man, who are you?

Kirzai did not answer. He did not know what to do. Should he tell the young man who he was, or say nothing about it?

Meanwhile the young man went on:

"In any case, you are not well. Where are you going?"

"To Givah," Kirzai replied. "But I have no more water."

Kirzai saw that the young man was weighing the situation to himself and he knew exactly what was going through his mind: should he help Kirzai or continue on his own business? But Kirzai also knew what the decision would be and he smiled as he watched the young man offering him a drink of water. The young man then filled his empty gourd, helped him up on his camel and pointed his finger:

"Go straight ahead that way and you'll be in Givah within two hours."

The old Kirzai looked a long moment at the young man he had once been and made a sign of acknowledgment to him. He would have wished to speak to the young man of many things, but he could only find these words:

"One day the desert will repay you."

And then he hastened off to Givah where his son awaited him.

Kirzai grew to be a wise man, respected by all. And when he would tell his strange tale, everyone who heard it believed him. Ever since that time the desert of Syr Darya had been known by the name Samovstrecha which means: the desert where one meets oneself.

ANOTHER KIND OF REMEMBERING

This is a story to live with. We must not try to understand it too quickly. But only note the ripple of feeling it may have evoked. This kind of feeling is rarely met with in our day-to-day lives, and our artists and musicians seem to know little about it. It is a feeling that involves an entirely new sense of relationship to oneself. This kind of relationship—along with this kind of feeling—has existed in our childhood. And if we can calmly let our earlier memories appear, we may realize that this feeling and this relationship were there in our *infancy,* before we knew words and names. Such memories are very delicate and subtle—they are not the violent memories of trauma that modern psychology emphasizes. They are memories of another vibration of perception that is part of our deeper minds. Such perceptions do not exist in time as we know it. And when we remember them we are not, strictly speaking, returning to a vanished past. No: *such remembering is the act of stepping out of time, as we know it, altogether!* But who is there to instruct us about this kind of remembering?

This is not familiar, psychological remembering; it is what we may call metaphysical remembering. Psychological remembering would take us into the vanished past. Metaphysical remembering takes us to a "place" where what we call time no longer exists, opening us to moments when capacities in us that operate outside of ordinary time come into contact with capacities that operate in causal, mechanical time.

The extraordinary quality of feeling we are speaking of is experienced when these two levels of perception come closer to each other within ourselves.

Many spiritual philosophers, poets and teachers speak of man as a two-natured being, within whom two disparate realities are meant to blend. The meaning of our lives cannot be understood, we are told, without the struggle to embrace these two realities together. These two realities are sometimes called time and eternity. The human self, as Kierkegaard expressed it, is created to hold together the infinite and the finite, the temporal and the eternal.[4] The special quality of feeling that the story of Kirzai can evoke is an echo of the special quality of feeling that all of us have known at the moments in our childhood *when consciousness first spoke its name,* which is precisely the experience of this uniquely human embrace that contains two worlds.

We are obsessed and paralyzed by time because we live in only one world, the world of visible matter and mechanical causality punctuated by accident. The world of visible matter is a world of ever accelerating causality and the proliferation of things and events. That world, according to the ancient teaching, is such that time must run ever faster and faster until death.

There is another world, another reality, where what we call time does not hold sway. It is not that time as such no longer exists, but it does not obey the same laws as the one world we live in now. From the perspective of the world we know, the process of time in this other world has the aspect of eternity.

But when these two worlds meet, or come closer to each other, that is the unique world of man, the world in which the eternal touches the temporal, where the changeless touches that which is ever changing in the direction of death. When the eternal and the temporal meet the result is what has been known in all traditional cultures as the *cycle of time.* The timeless and the temporal meet in the reality of rhythm and recurrence. When we genuinely experience the sense of recurrence and rep-

etition in our life, it brings a taste of this unique feeling
we are speaking of: we are personally verifying the truth
of the idea of cycle, rhythm and recurrence.

But before examining this aspect of our moments of
uniquely human feeling, it is necessary to return to the
act of allowing in the subtle memories of infancy when
consciousness first alighted in us, as it were, from within
our uniquely human brain and mind. Do you remember?
Can you remember *when you were first there?* Do you
remember—and the novelist, the talespinner, hears a fictional character saying it, urging it in a way a mere writer
of philosophical prose cannot allow himself.

"Search, Eliot! Go back in time. Collect yourself,
become quiet. Remember. . . ."

The speaker is an old man with a frail body and powerful, dark eyes. The scene is a modest apartment over-
looking the Schuylkill River in Philadelphia. Dr. Appleman has been summoned from far away to visit this man
who meant so much to him so many years ago, and who
is now waiting to die. Or so the letter had said. But looking at the old man now, his leonine head bathed in the
fiery amber-gold light of the setting October sun,
Dr. Appleman senses nothing of illness or death in his old
teacher.

When he was fifteen years old, Eliot had fallen in with
a group of teenage boys studying stage magic. On Satur-
days the young Eliot would hurry downtown to the sleek
world of Templeton's Magic Shop to watch the squat fig-
ure of Max Falkoner, the consummate pitchman and

sleight-of-hand artist, hold dominion from behind the counter, his eyes squinting in the smoke of a dangling cigarette. But behind the mask, as Eliot soon discovered, was an uncompromising teacher of awakening truth, a combination of showman, sage and master magician.

The novel will only give hints of what the fifteen-year-old Eliot learned from this man, only enough to set the scene where the aging teacher sends Dr. Appleman back in time. The reader needs to know only that Max Falkoner speaks from a source of knowledge about man and the universe that is very little known to our present world, a source from which the sacred teachings of mankind have drawn their life. *This* idea is not fiction. There has existed such a source. The novelist himself, a student and scholar of the history of religions, has verified this. But that is another story . . . or is it? Perhaps it is the same story.

From the first moment, this scene between the aging teacher and Dr. Appleman is meant to let the reader feel that only another kind and *level* of knowledge can help us face the mystery of time.

Dr. Appleman begins by smiling to himself indulgently at the fact that the old man is asking *him*, the skilled psychiatrist, to remember his past. Obviously Max is not aware of the profession Eliot entered in the years that have gone by. Not only has Dr. Appleman himself gone through a long, extensive psychoanalysis as part of his training, but in the course of his career he has guided hundreds of men and women through the process of remembering their pasts. The practice of remembering the past is his stock in trade, it is what he knows best and it is what he has built his professional reputation upon. He has even published books about it.

THE GIFTS OF TIME

I want the scene to hit fairly hard on this point—that Eliot naively imagines he understands more about remembering than his old teacher. Eliot has completely forgotten the kind of power that he once saw in Max Falkoner's words and actions. Neither does it even occur to him—except fleetingly and vaguely—to wonder that he has been called to see Max at this particular moment in his own life, a moment when his whole future is at stake, the facade of his marriage crumbling away, the facade of his way of caring for his children crumbling away and his self-important fantasies about helping others and understanding the mind unraveling to the point where he is staring into an abyss of loneliness, meaninglessness and self-dissolution. The distinguished Dr. Appleman, healer of souls, begins to realize that he himself is a sick man. It never occurs to Dr. Appleman that his old teacher may know this about him. It never occurs to Dr. Appleman that his life has been watched from afar.

Just as it never occurs to any of us that compassion is an objective property of reality. I want the novel to open this idea here—although not too explicitly. But I want the reader to sense that there is a kind of love that the universe is constantly offering us, if only we knew how to receive it or even ask for it. Once we really ask, it is immediately given.

Some wisdom teachings say that our very life itself is just such an answer. Our birth and the events of our life, we are sometimes told, are just such an answer, such a gift. But we have forgotten how to receive this gift. The trauma of birth and early childhood has driven our need and our question back down into the dark waters of forgetfulness. And all the gifts that time offers us are wasted upon us; we do not take them in; we do not digest our lives. The food of time is wasted upon us.

But when he was young Eliot asked, Eliot questioned. At the age of fifteen he pursues a teenage boy's fantasy of learning magic, but that fantasy reflects a desire to go beneath the surface of so-called logic and so-called reality. And his attraction to Max reveals that his desire is more than an adolescent boy's fantasy. Max shows Eliot himself. He shows him his self and lets him glimpse the inner truth about man that must be worked for with all the diligence and courage that a human being is capable of.

The young Eliot forgot that question and that search as he lawfully was drawn into the world of sex and career and all the necessary illusions that fuel the life of man on earth and that serve as the medium through which the gifts of time are offered. Eliot forgot. And time passed. And at the age of fifty, when he knows in his bones that he has nowhere to go but down to destruction, he is called back. Because he once asked the question he is called back to meet himself. The desert will repay him.

CHAPTER 4

TIME AND THE
GREAT SELF

When I dream of how the old teacher speaks to Eliot Appleman, I can't help thinking as well of one of the greatest examples in world literature of a teacher of wisdom speaking to a troubled seeker. In the Bhagavad Gita, the most widely revered sacred text of India, the warrior Arjuna stands before a field of battle. The enemies arrayed before him are his own kinsmen and teachers. Thousands stand on either side: horses, chariots and great warrior elephants are poised to advance; bronze shields and drawn swords catch the first rays of the morning sun; the rising wind lifts a thousand terrifying banners and the urgent cry of the ancient conch pierces the air; ten thousand arrows are poised to fly.

THE DEJECTION OF ARJUNA

When the warrior realizes whom he must fight, when he deeply feels what he only knew in his mind, that he is called to do battle with his own kinsmen, he draws his chariot to a halt. His blood is chilled. He cannot move.

The warrior is overcome by grief and despair and speaks to his charioteer, who is none other than Krishna, God, Lord of the Universe.

> "When I see all of my kinsmen, Krishna, who have
>   come here on this field of battle,
> Life goes from my lips and they sink, and my mouth
>   is sere and dry. . . .
> My great bow Gandiva falls down from my
>   hands . . .
> Facing us in the field of battle are teachers,
>   fathers, and sons;
>   grandsons, grandfathers, wives, brothers . . .
> These I do not wish to slay, even if I myself
>   am slain. . . .
> What evil spirit moved our minds when for
>   the sake of an earthly kingdom
>   we came to this field of battle ready to kill
>   our own people?"

Here the narrator tells us:

Thus spoke Arjuna in the field of battle, and letting fall his bow and arrows he sank down in his chariot, his soul overcome by grief and despair.

He is answered by the Lord God Krishna. Even after a hundred readings of this text, Krishna's first words to Arjuna evoke astonishment. What kind of a God is it who urges not love and peace but war and conflict?

> "Whence this lifeless dejection, Arjuna, in this hour of trial? Strong men know not despair, Arjuna, for this wins neither heaven nor earth. Fall not into degrading weakness . . . and arise like a fire that burns all before it."[5]

But Arjuna repeats his lament. Again he speaks of those he is about to fight and kill—all these men with whom he grew up and from whom he learned about life, all those whom he cared for and who cared for him. As he speaks, the master hand of the poet begins to lift the veil of the great allegory; who are these people of Arjuna's past, and who is Arjuna who stands now on the field of battle? What are his tears? What is the sense of his anxiety and sorrow?

As a novelist, as a spinner of tales, I see the meeting between the metaphysical teacher and the psychiatrist capturing its light from the immense sun of this ancient Oriental drama. The psychiatrist wants to remember all the things that have shaped his life, he wants to go back to a past inhabited by his mother and father or even beyond.

But there is another past and another remembering of which the psychiatrist knows nothing. Fight, Arjuna!

"Remember, Eliot, remember . . ."

"But I am remembering, Max. I can practically touch my mother and father, I can see. . . ."

"You see nothing, Eliot. You see only shadows, ghosts."

"I see myself as a young man. I remember, *clearly*, what I felt and thought, I see. . . ."

"You see nothing, Eliot. You see nothing of yourself. You see only a phantom. Remember . . . remember. . . ."

What is Max talking about? What relationship to time does he represent? The answer is both simple and awesome. We cannot live in human time without first struggling to become human ourselves. We have become things, objects, clocks, watches, computers, springs and wheels and boxes and plastic and metal; our attention, the most precious part of a human being, is spilled into the objects of our world like water spilled into the burning sand of the Syr Darya desert.

In the Bhagavad Gita, Krishna answers the dejection of Arjuna by speaking the name of the great self within, *Atman.* He is directing Arjuna to an entirely new kind of attention within himself that transcends all limitations of time and anxiety.

The poet now lifts the veil halfway. Although he is still speaking in the imagery of external warfare, we who read the text begin to hear the ancient instruction given since the beginning of human history to all men and women who seek the eternal in the midst of time. Seen through the half-lifted veil, where the allegorical symbols are peeling away to reveal the One Truth, the words of God to Arjuna may at first seem troubling or even repugnant:

> "Thy tears are for those beyond tears. . . . The wise grieve not for those who live; and they grieve not for those who die—for life and death shall pass away.

"Because we all have been for all time; I and thou, and those kings of men. And we all shall be for all time, we all for ever and ever. . . . The unreal never is: the Real never is not. This truth indeed has been seen by those who can see the true.

"For beyond time he [the Eternal] dwells in these bodies, though these bodies have their end in their time. . . . Therefore, great warrior, carry on thy fight.

"If any man thinks he slays, and if another thinks he is slain, neither knows the ways of truth. The Eternal in man cannot kill: the Eternal in man cannot die. . . .

"Beyond the power of sword and fire, beyond the power of waters and winds, the Atman is everlasting, omnipresent, never-changing, never-moving, ever One. . . .

"Invisible before birth are all beings and after death invisible again. They are seen between two unseens. Why in this truth find sorrow? . . .

"There is a war that opens the doors of Heaven, Arjuna! Happy the warriors whose fate is to fight such a war."

The idea of the greater self within is not meant only as a comforting thought to which we turn in times of difficulty. Neither, under certain readings, is the Christian idea of man's immortal soul meant solely as such a comfort. The deeper meaning of these ideas is that here and now in this life, with all its pressure and suffering, there can exist a deep sensibility that reconciles and transforms the anxieties of our life in time. But this quality of attention has been forgotten, as has the specific inner struggle that can allow it to come into our awareness.

How to communicate Eliot's difficulty in understanding what his teacher is demanding of him? Max is calling Eliot to remember in himself something that necessarily includes but goes far beyond the events and emotions of his childhood. He is calling him to remember what the Zen Buddhists call the "original face," the self he was "before he was born." You and I, reader, may take this kind of expression as metaphor, as an intriguing poetic manner of speaking about a kind of experience we can readily acknowledge and value. But it is not so. It is not metaphor. There is a face within us, a source of attention and consciousness, that is eternal. It is a literal fact. A material fact. To treat it as a metaphor for something we readily understand is to commit a kind of spiritual suicide. The metaphysical cemeteries are filled with graves of scholars and poets and artists—brilliant, learned, full of heartfelt subjective conviction—who grasped this idea too easily, too cleverly, who absorbed it into their sense-based, logico-imaginative reasoning where the assumptions are childish, one-eyed, and the chain of logical deduction phenomenally ingenious, and the conclusion toxic to the point of locking us more securely in the prison of time and neurosis. If we are not astonished by the idea of this kind of remembering, then we have not begun to understand it. If we imagine we can carry out this demand to remember our eternal self, if we think this remembering is something we can *do*, we have not begun to understand it.

PART II

REAL TIME

CHAPTER 5

FROM FICTION TO REALITY

There is a life I wish to live. It is not a life with different events or different people than make up the life I am now living. It is not a life where things have come out differently, with fewer defeats or greater triumphs. It is not a life with fewer mistakes. No. It is this life, my actual life. It is *this* life that I wish to live, the same life I am living, but with one great difference: a difference in the experience of time.

The fact is that I am not now living my life—it is living me. I am not—as used to be said—conducting my affairs; they are conducting me, driving *me*. And with ever increasing acceleration and tempo.

THE TIME FAMINE

I am having dinner with a brilliant and devoted doctor. He is well known for having introduced revolutionary patient-care procedures in one of the country's most prestigious medical centers. When I remark about the success of his work and ask about its future, his dark eyes suddenly well up with tears! Is he becoming emotional because of the deep feeling he has for his work or his patients? Not exactly. He puts down his cup and in an unsteady voice that is part desperation and part anger he says:

"I have no time."

I nod sympathetically. But he goes on:

"You don't understand. I have no time! I am pathologically busy. It's beyond anything I have ever imagined. I can't give anything the attention it needs. I can't do anything well. I wake up in the middle of the night on the verge of a breakdown. And more and more people depend on me. More and more things, good things, important things, keep coming to me. Any one of them is worth the whole of my attention and needs my time. But ten, twenty of them? A hundred of them? And it is the same with my staff. They are being driven past their limits. . . ."

My friend keeps talking, talking. I cannot find a moment to break in to say, "Yes, I understand. It's the same with me."

Here is an old friend of mine who runs an art gallery in Vancouver. I have always admired his attitude toward life's difficulties and losses. He has invariably met them with an extraordinary composure. It has been less than six months since I last saw him, yet now, as we are just beginning to greet each other and ask about each other's well-being, he speaks with completely uncharacteristic anxiety. "I feel I have sold my soul to the devil," he says. "I really must calm down. I have to stop traveling around so much. Doing so much. I really can't bear what is happening."

This man is what the world would consider an exceptionally strong, balanced being, as is the doctor I just quoted. I could cite countless other examples—men, women, *children!* Rich, poor, middle class. In America, Europe, Asia, Africa. I am not speaking of fragile people, of people without what passes for will power, education, depth of mind and heart. I am not speaking of people consumed by personal ambition, or of people who seek mainly to make money or become more "effective." I am speaking, I believe, of some of the most devoted and talented people in our society—extremely able people who care greatly for others and who willingly sacrifice their own immediate good for the benefit of others. And I am speaking of people who, underneath it all, are searching for Truth, the Truth that transcends what the world offers as wealth, safety and virtue. Many of them are followers of one or another spiritual practice, many of them are not. But it is safe to say that none of them really believes in the world as it presents itself; it is safe to say that all of them suspect, suspect . . . that there exists a great secret behind the appearances of our world, and that there exists a great secret beyond the appearances of themselves. It is not only the tempo of their lives that is driving them mad, it is the sense that they are not living their lives. With all the best intentions in the world, and with all the best efforts that they can muster, still they have been drawn, they do not know how, into an unreal life. It is not their own life they are living.

This is not my life. How did this happen? What does it mean? Is it possible that time has become what it has only because our lives are submerged in lies?

Perhaps I can glimpse this strange truth more clearly when I look into the eyes of the doctor. I know that the great crises of my own life show me I am living in lies—about myself, my relationships, my abilities and powers. But I don't see these lies very clearly—I only sense them. I know they are there. Could it be that time is racing because I have been lying to myself?

Nowhere has this idea ever been explored—at least not in these words: that the experience of time depends entirely on the degree to which one is either aware of truth or pursuing a lie. We need to examine this new idea. There is hope in it. It is possible we have discovered a chink in the armor of time and its implacability: it is because of our lies and self-deceptions that time devours us! Or, to put it more positively and in words that can echo the ancient wisdom: Truth conquers time—*Truth is eternal.*

Let us go slowly and return to the doctor and the art dealer and the time-famine that is epidemic in our society. Almost all of us are gasping for more time. We are starving. And all the devices and techniques that our inventive culture offers only increase the yearning for time—like the food of hell that makes the eater hungrier. Our cell phones, computers and fax machines and the countless other inventions that "save time" only starve us more and more, exactly like the food of hell. We are paying for these things with our time, with our lives, which is our time.

Slowly, let us think s-l-o-w-l-y. Consider this famine and the men and women who suffer from it most painfully, many of whom are the best hearts and minds among us. They do not need and do not want what is called "time management." This whole problem goes far beyond self-help books and methods. No seminar, no sectioning of one's life into quadrants, nothing one can put down on paper or on a spreadsheet is the answer to our hunger for time. Even methods borrowed from ancient traditions, including the great words of the wise—"be here, now, in the present moment," "relax," "meditate"—by themselves offer only temporary help. It is not hard to see through such methods and programs, which tend to make us imagine we can improve a metaphysical situation by psychosocial methods invented or adapted by the very kind of mentality through which the whole problem of time has first appeared. Psychological technologies are not the answer to the problems created by electronic technologies. And the reason they are not the answer is, in part, that psychological technologies are themselves based on a surface truth that conceals a deep lie. It seems, at the surface of our lives, that we can change ourselves by ourselves. But, under the surface, Truth is smiling at us, sorrowfully. We do not have to live very long before we discover that, under the surface of all our manipulations, our situation remains the same; we have done little more than move a few pieces of furniture within the four walls of our prison. Self-help methods are part of the American dream, but at the level at which the power of time operates, at the deep metaphysical level of the being of man, self-help methods are powerless. At this level—call it, if you like, the cosmic level, the level at which the very fact of human existence and death are at issue—it is an entirely new energy that must enter into the psyche.

Our relationship to time is what it is because we lie to ourselves about what we are and what we can do and we hide from ourselves what we are meant to be and what we are meant to serve. If we look carefully and quietly at the great teachings of wisdom, we can detect this message at the core of their doctrines and symbols. "Self-help" changes nothing at the core of our being. Something far deeper and far more mysterious needs to enter into us. The time-famine of our lives and our culture is in fact a symptom of a metaphysical starvation. But it is also a sign that the transformation of human nature is possible: as the wise have said, the laws of justice decree that whatever is necessary for man is possible for him.

The philosopher writes about such ideas and the novelist dramatizes them, but who can say he understands them?

The new mind, the new life that needs to enter us, is simply incomprehensible to the old mind by which we "conduct" our lives. The social self cannot understand the great Self. It cannot believe in it. The old mind, the mind that is trapped in time, can by its own efforts only succeed, at best, in making the trap bigger, vaster, more comfortable. Yet the old mind must let go of its imaginary powers—not so much in the outer world where we do our business and care for our needs and responsibilities, but in the inner, causal world, in which we can open to another reality and through which this new reality can enter our bodies and our lives. We are speaking, once again, of the incomprehensible meeting of time and eternity. The old mind, the social self, needs to remember . . . remember. . . .

I want to show Eliot Appleman, the skilled psychiatrist, utterly baffled by what his old teacher is demanding of him. As a psychiatrist, he represents our culture's best understanding of the mind, but that understanding stands helpless before the vision of consciousness that calls to us from the hidden teachings of wisdom and for the hidden depths of ourselves.

"Max, what are you asking me? What am I supposed to remember? I *am* remembering! I see myself very clearly. . . ."

"You see nothing," says Max. "*You* are not remembering. *You* are not seeing!"

"Max, I don't know what you're talking about! What are you trying to do to me?"

THE INSTRUCTIONS OF HERMES

I want this scene to echo far back to an extraordinary sdialogue written down in Alexandrian Egypt nearly two thousand years ago. In a body of writings known as the *Corpus Hermeticum*[6] we find the traces of an authentic school of inner wisdom, which greatly influenced the subsequent history of Western philosophy and science. Many of these texts take the form of a dialogue between the legendary master, Hermes Trismegistus (Thrice-Greatest Hermes), and his son Tat. Here, the pupil, Tat, is asking his father to explain more clearly the doctrine of *palingenesis*—a Greek word that means, literally, *to begin again*, and that is customarily translated as *rebirth*. Like Eliot Appleman, who is about to be sent back in time in order to begin again through a mysterious process of remembering, Tat pleads with his mythical father and teacher:

". . . Father, you spoke in riddles when discussing the divine nature in man, for merely to say that no one can be free unless he is born again *(palingenesis)* explains nothing.

". . . I do not know from what nature of womb man is born again, nor from what kind of seed."

Hermes answers that the teachings of wisdom are the nourishing womb and that the seed of the new beginning is that which is truly good, the true aim for a human being.

"But how is this seed sown in a man?" Tat asks. "I cannot understand at all."

"It is sown in us by the will of God," Hermes replies.

Tat's puzzlement deepens. But why is he puzzled by a reply like this, which on the surface seems to be nothing more than a conventionally religious answer? To say the seed of a new life is sown in man by the will of God must have been then, as it is now, such an oft-repeated kind of phrase that by itself it could not be a "puzzle" to anyone. Then why is Tat bewildered? The answer must be that the teacher is speaking not of some cliché-ridden concept of an external God but of a great and incomprehensible presence within man himself, within Tat, the pupil, himself. The teacher is tearing away the pupil's sense of who and what he is.

One can almost hear Tat's voice rising as he cries out, "What manner of man can be born again? What kind of self?"

The teacher answers, holding steady to the vision of selfhood that overturns everything we understand about ourselves:

"Only a man who is a son of God, serving God's will."

There exists a selfhood that is open to the highest life in the universe. But it is not the self you think you are. It is not the self you remember or the self that tries to remember.

"What is a man like when he is reborn?" Tat asks, desperately trying to follow.

Hermes answers, "He that is born by that birth is another being; he is a god, and son of God. His self is now the All that is in all. His self is composed of a completely new substance or energy unlike the materiality of the bodies and things of the world we see and live in."

This is too much for the ancient pupil, too much for Eliot Appleman, too much for all of us who are trapped in time . . . time that is the sum of all the lies about what we are and are meant to be.

"Your words have no meaning," says Tat, "they are mere riddles. You are not speaking to me as a father should speak to a son!"

But Hermes does not give up. The teacher continues, without compromise, to guide the pupil toward the surrender of his tense efforts to think his way to Truth. The teacher guides the pupil in the act of loosening the reins of thought and allowing the mind to open to what is calling to us from another part of the mind. The teacher guides the pupil in the process of remembering.

"This kind of thing cannot be taught, my son; but God, when He so wills, recalls it to our memory."

"Father," says Tat, "what you are speaking of is impossible. It does violence to everything that is rational. When you treat me like this, I have every right to ask if I have suddenly become a stranger to my father's race. Do not grudge me this. I am your true-born son! Explain to me what it means to be born again!"

"What more can I say to you, my son? This thing cannot be taught and it is not possible for you to grasp it in the way you are trying. I can only tell you this. . . ."

And here the master speaks of himself and what he is, but it is clear that he is speaking of the deep self within ourselves, the self that every man or woman is called to remember:

"I see that by God's mercy something new has been born in me, and I have passed forth out of myself into an immortal body [a body not subject to time]. I am not now the man I was; I have been reborn in Mind and the body which was mine before no longer forms my identity. No longer am I something that can be touched by the hand or seen by the eyes or measured in space. I am now separate and other than all this, and a stranger to all that you perceive by gazing with your eyes. To such eyes as yours, my son, I am not now visible."

What is Tat to say to this?

"Father," he replies, his own eyes wide with disbelief, "you have driven me to raving madness. Are you actually telling me that I do not at this moment see my own self?"

The teacher answers:

"Would that you too, my son, were separated from yourself and could see, not as men and women see who dream in sleep, but as one awake."

"What are you saying?" Tat stammers again. "I am looking right at you! I see you right here before me! I see your form and features the same as ever!"

"Even in this you are mistaken, my son. The physical body you see changes from moment to moment under the sway of time. It is not real."

What we know as time is but the sum of all the lies we live by.

Tat bows his head.

"What then is real, thrice-greatest one?"

Again Hermes answers by speaking of the great Self within, which transcends all that we can define by our logic and our external senses and whose central property is consciousness and understanding. It can be known only by itself. It is not subject to time as we know it. And this reality alone is what man is meant to be; in this lies our own authentic good.

"I must be going insane," Tat cries out. "I thought your teaching was bringing me wisdom. But when you speak like this it is as though I had lost all my wits and senses!"

"With your wits and senses," Hermes replies, "you might as well be deaf and blind. That which is beyond your logic and sense perception cannot be apprehended in this way. Another kind of seeing is needed, not what you call thought and perception."

Tat becomes quiet. "Is it then beyond my power, Father?"

Here we may imagine the legendary teacher pausing and then speaking in a new way. He sees that the pupil has been brought to the threshold of understanding and can now be guided in the actual inner search that leads to remembering the Self. Tat has asked if this remembering is beyond his power. "May it be not so, my son," Hermes answers. And now he instructs his pupil to begin the process of recalling his attention from its immersion in the physical and emotional reactions proceeding in his presence. "Bring your attention into yourself and allow this capacity to appear in you. Wish for it and it will come. Separate yourself from the working of your reactions and senses so that God may be born in you. You must free yourself from the inner torments of the heavy matter within you."

"What do you mean, Father? Have I torturers within me?"

"Yes, my son, and not a few; they are terrible and they are many."

"I do not know them, Father."

"This very ignorance, my son," says Hermes, "is one of the torments."

After more words of this kind, there is a break in the ancient text. We are, as it were, asked to pause; and when the text resumes, it is as though a great period of silence has passed between teacher and pupil. Is it fifteen minutes of silence and quiet inner searching—or an hour? Or months—or years of specific, concrete guided inner searching that cannot and must not be written down or needlessly spoken?

However that may be, the teacher's next words show that the pupil has in fact, in actual experience, touched the new birth:

"Rejoice now, my son; you are being worked upon and purified by divine forces; for they have come to build up in you the body made of Mind. . . ."

"Father," says the pupil, "God has made me a new being, and I perceive things now, not with bodily eyesight, but with the energies of mind."

"This is what it means," Hermes replies, "to be born again (*palingenesis*, to begin again), when not only the body with its three dimensions is visible, but also the new body made of Mind [the new Self]."

"Father," says Tat in calm tones of wonder, "now that I see in Mind, I see myself to be the All. I am in heaven and in earth, in water and in air; I am in beasts and plants; I am a babe in the womb, and one that is not yet conceived, and one that has been born; I am present everywhere."

To this Hermes answers simply:

"Now, my son, you know what the Rebirth is."

Such texts as these—and there are many—invariably drive home one central idea about the structure of human nature: we are not what we think we are. We live our lives—we think, feel and act—on the surface of ourselves, on the surface of an immensity that, were we to experience it, would answer all our questions and purify all the suffering of our lives. This immensity has many names. But we can call it the *Self.*

Even the religions that emphasize the existence of an external God above in whom man must believe and hope are in their way pointing us toward this greater Self within. The mystery of the external God is what it is because of the mystery of what is in ourselves. The way of prayer, for example, is its depths, is calling for men and women to search in themselves for a mind and heart that is capable of yearning for God, capable of asking that He do *His* will and not necessarily what we, in our surface self, wish for. Such capacities, the capacity to ask nonegoistically and to separate from one's most intense personal desires—such capacities are already steppingstones on the way to the great Self within, what is called spirit or the higher soul in the mystical traditions of Judaism, Christianity and Islam.

How does this teaching help us understand why we are trapped by time? The main point is that in our ignorance about ourselves we are living inside a great falsehood. We imagine that we are already that which we can be only through remembering the Self. We act as though we are already eternal beings. We plan, we fight, we rejoice, we make and "do" as though we are already eternal beings. That is, we do not remember, *we do not sense or feel* the transitory nature of everything we give ourselves to in our day-to-day lives. Most importantly, we do not sense or feel the transitoriness of our own being.

This sounds paradoxical. Aren't we so driven by our lives just because we realize how fleeting and fragile they are? Don't we worry about things and people precisely because we realize how they are subject to change and destruction? Aren't we trying to touch something, anything, in our lives and our relationships that can withstand the relentless transitoriness of it all?

But consider. Consider the way we imagine that we know something is right or wrong, or that someone has done us good or harm. Consider how we feel ourselves when we vehemently judge that something has gone wrong, that we have made a mistake that must be corrected immediately. Can we really say we are aware of the real significance, objectively speaking, of the thing or event that suddenly looms up as so important and that takes from us all our available energy of attention? Driven by needlessly intense emotional reactions to whatever "presses our buttons," we forget not only what we are and are meant to be, we forget the actual significance of the thing that is troubling us. More often than not, after a few hours or days, or even after a few moments, we "recover" and realize that, in the words of G. I. Gurdjieff, we have "made an elephant out of a fly." This continual and endless process of reaction and recovery uses up our psychic energy and our allotted time. And as we examine this process dispassionately we may come to see that time is energy—not physical energy, but psychic energy. When we contain our psychic energy we experience the adequacy of time; when we squander our psychic energy we squander time. And we squander our psychic energy because we do not sense and feel the transitoriness and relative insignificance of the things and events that draw us so far out of ourselves. We squander our time because we do not remember the truth about ourselves or about the world in front of us.

THE THIEVES OF TIME

Each little "self" within us—and they are many—has the power to take away a portion of our time. These "selves" do this again and again, over and over, as we repeatedly act out the limited number of inner and outer scenarios that make up our lives. It is the defining essence of our neurosis that we continually and mechanically repeat these scenarios. And that *we* are not *there* to witness them. The teachings of wisdom tell us that these scenarios take from us the time and the psychic energy that are given to human beings in order to form within ourselves a presence, a selfhood, that can become free of the tyranny of time—a presence that can, as is said in some teachings, even survive the fate of the physical body.

Let us be clear what we mean when we speak of these lesser "selves" and their scenarios. We are speaking first of all of what are now sometimes called the negative emotions: fear, guilt, self-pity, hurt feelings, anger, lovesickness and many others. All of us are prey to these emotions, though individuals differ as to which of them predominate. Some of us are almost always nursing some hurt or slight; others are continually angry or irritated, whether we express this anger or only live it in our thoughts; others fall from one occasion for self-pity to another; others are constantly guilty about things big and small, from their family relationships or mankind and the earth itself to their cat or dog or even a plant that needs watering.

The list of these emotions is endless and fascinating to consider. Ancient teachings spoke of the seven deadly sins, but what is deadly about them is not so much the harm they may bring to others, but the harm they bring to oneself. And the harm they bring to oneself includes the power they seem to have to take from us our most precious inner poverty—our specifically human time and attention. These deadly sins, these devouring emotions, repeat and repeat and repeat. And at the end of these repetitions nothing is left of ourselves, nothing has been brought into ourselves. To begin again *(palingenesis)* does not mean destroying these reactions; it means removing from them their power to take us away from ourselves.

At a more obvious level, these reactions, by drawing away our attention and influencing the direction of our thought and perception, continually lead us into decisions and situations that we sooner or later realize do not correspond to what we want or need and that take a great deal of time and energy to deal with. Time and again we find ourselves in the same kind of difficulty, surrounded by the same kind of events, the same kind of people—the same betrayals, the same heartbreak, the same kind of loss in business or romance, the same petty crime or hollow triumph, the same kind of "wrong" man or woman, making the same mistake with our parents or children. And again and again spending time and energy correcting the situation, which leaves us, in the end, at more or less the same point at which we started—often making vain and powerless promises to ourselves about doing better the next time. It sometimes happens, of course, that one spends one's whole life trying to set right just one of the situations that result from these reactions. One is constantly sweeping away the leaves that are always falling and never actually setting off on the path that the leaves keep covering. Thus do we squander our time, our lives.

CHAPTER 6

WHAT TO DO?

What to do? It is that question that sends Eliot back in time to accompany himself as an adolescent at the threshold of manhood. In no way can he understand what Max means by remembering. Like the ancient pupil Tat standing before his teacher Hermes, Eliot finally bows his head in sorrow. "Max," he says softly, "I can't understand. What you're asking is completely beyond my power." And just as Hermes replies to Tat, Max answers, in his own idiom: "Cut it out, Appleman! Try . . . try. . . ." Wasn't it Krishna himself, lord of the universe, who rebuked the warrior Arjuna for his sadness and his unwillingness to engage in a struggle he does not yet understand: "Why this lifeless dejection, Arjuna? . . . Fall not into this degrading weakness. . . . Fight, Arjuna!"

The emotional reactions that devour our time are only the most obvious evidence that our relationship to time depends primarily on our inner state and not on any objective characteristics of time itself. We are called to a struggle we do not yet understand; and therefore our first task is to try to see why, in spite of this, we must begin this incomprehensible work, this effort to remember the Self. When man is closer to the Self, time is no longer the enemy, so we are told by the ancient wisdom. It is the man who is less than Man whom time mercilessly destroys. It is the self that is less than the Self that is devoured by time.

But it is clear that the effort we need to make cannot be explained in words; otherwise the pupil would not be bowing his head before the teacher or the god. The understanding that we need cannot come through ideas or doctrines alone. We must *try* something. But what?

Nor, as has already been said, can techniques or methods by themselves be of help. Not even methods borrowed from sacred sources and applied as a form of psychological technology. We can recite mantras and meditate and "be here now." But who is meditating? Who is reciting the mantra? What does he or she want? To "save time" or to understand? Time cannot be "saved." It can only be given—and given, so we are told, as a result of the mysterious effort to understand the truth and serve the good within ourselves and within the universal world. To try to save time, to try to get time, is as futile as trying to *get* happiness, that happiness which is not pleasure but an abiding sense of meaning and well-being. Such things are given, not taken. But in order to receive, the hand needs to be open. What we are speaking of here are efforts that can open a man or woman to the great winds of conscious, enduring selfhood.

We need a new way to approach the aspects of our inner lives that destroy or degrade time. What does wisdom tell us about worry and anxiety, for example, or busyness or daydreaming or the countless other manifestations of men and women like ourselves who have forgotten our essential being? Perhaps there is no Krishna or Hermes in front of us urging us to remember the Self within us. But there do exist the teachings of wisdom that have been handed down from one generation to another behind the scenes of the mad theater of human history. Can these teachings help us to understand what really steals from us the time that we have been given? And can we hear a voice calling to us from the source of these ancient truths—the voice not of a mythic or fictional teacher, but our own voice, our own Self, calling us to . . . to what? To remember? Or . . . *to be remembered?*

ON BEING TOO BUSY

When I was a teenage boy and was precociously trying to read the great philosophers, I once came upon a statement attributed to Aristotle: "The wise man is never in a hurry." I remember putting the book down and then picking it up and reading the sentence over and over again. What did it mean? What did being in a hurry have to do with being wise? I understood that a wise man would be compassionate, would not be mean, vain or petty; that he would understand deep truths about life and death and the universe, would not crave fame or riches or pleasure. But why this "not be in a hurry"? Wasn't a wise man ever late? Did he or she never have to run for a bus?

I was puzzled and fascinated. I felt there was some great truth in this idea, but it seemed very different from all the other characteristics of wisdom. This idea of never being in a hurry was actually something I could immediately apply to myself, something I could try to do. It was—or so it seemed—something that could actually bring me one step closer to becoming wise. The other attributes of wisdom—compassion and great knowledge and self-denial—were all well and good as ideals, things to dream about, things to inspire one. But they had nothing to do with any action I could take—in fact, that was part of *their* attraction, that was part of their consolation in difficult moments. But this "not be in a hurry" presented itself immediately as something I could do.

I think of myself in those days as being very much like young Eliot Appleman, which is to say that part of a man or woman that stands at the threshold of adulthood—and not merely biological or social adulthood. I wanted very much to grow up, to care for things that were real, to give my time and effort to things that were real—not just to games or fantasies, and not just to running round and round fleeing from imaginary fears and exaggerated discomforts. Instinctively, I sensed that this effort to "not be in a hurry" would help me to be more like a grown-up man.

So I tried. Again and again, I would catch myself hurrying here or there without any real need for haste or, for that matter, without any real awareness of what I was doing at all. When I caught myself like this I would immediately slow down. Sometimes I would move as though in slow motion, wondering if people passing me would think I was mad. At meals I would chew slowly, one bite at a time, instead of stuffing food into an already full mouth. My mother and father did not seem to notice anything unusual; at least, they didn't say anything.

I distinctly remember one morning when I was late for school. As I was automatically rushing to get dressed and put my books together, I recalled Aristotle. But even as the aim of not being in a hurry came to me, my thoughts started to tell me that I mustn't try now or I would never be able to make the opening bell and would be marked late and . . . who knew what terrors would follow from that? At the same time, my mother was calling me to hurry up, reminding me that I would miss the streetcar, but that I still needed to eat some breakfast, but not gobble my food, but yet hurry up . . . et cetera.

What stands out in my mind, even after all these years, is the attitude I took toward my thoughts. I simply ignored them. I simply and swiftly ignored them. I did not argue with them and I did not look for other thoughts to put against them, such as the thought that there was still enough time, that I always got to school early or that even if I was late it wouldn't really make any difference, I could always make up an excuse and even one late mark didn't matter anyway . . . I did not bring forth any of these thoughts at all. I simply turned my attention away from all my thoughts. Suddenly, swiftly, gently, without bargaining with them at all. I calmly turned my attention to putting on my shoes and socks, tying my shoes, selecting my brown sweater, assembling my notebook and textbooks, walking into the kitchen, sitting down and eating the cornflakes. I was not thinking of anything at all except the shoes and socks, the sweater, the books, the cereal and milk. It seemed that, having made one big instantaneous decision not to pay attention to thoughts, my mind became a completely different kind of instrument, attending just enough to what was right in front of me and yet also holding an overall vision of what had to be done and when and for what purpose—namely, getting to school as quickly as possible.

As I was halfway through my breakfast, I realized that in fact I had been moving with great speed through everything. A certain feeling of joy started appearing at the back of my head and in my body. As I ran down the stairs and out the door, I realized that, although I was hurrying, there was not the slightest sense of tension or anxiety. I was moving fast, very fast, *but I was not in a hurry!* What would Aristotle have said to that? I wondered.

I raced down the Johnson Street hill to catch the streetcar, but I was not in a hurry. I felt I had plenty of time. And when, in fact, I missed the streetcar, it did not trouble me at all. I simply did what I had never before done in my life—I put out my thumb to hitchhike. I was picked up by a man driving a beautiful new car who delivered me in warm comfort even a few minutes ahead of the streetcar. Inside, I was laughing with elation.

Even then, although I had no words or ideas with which to grasp what was happening, I vaguely realized that I had become a completely different kind of person. I can say now more precisely what had taken place: to a small extent, something had appeared in myself that was a taste, a forerunner, of the Self. I was no longer just Jerry. Or, rather, I was Jerry grown up, awake, clear, relaxed, more intensely alive and sensitive, calling forth actions and capacities that I was not aware I had.

After this experience passed, I was no longer so sure about Aristotle or what he had meant. I continued trying to not be in a hurry (when I remembered to try), but it was not the same thing as before. When I intentionally slowed my movements while walking or eating, I did not have the same sense of inner freedom as that one experience had given me. On the contrary, the effort to slow down began to carry exactly as much tension as my usual impatience and impulses to hurry. Like all such piecemeal efforts, it gradually faded away from my life after becoming absorbed into my everyday personality.

It was only many years later that this exercise reappeared in my awareness. My life, like the lives of many men and women, had become filled with too many things to do, too many responsibilities, too many opportunities, too many important details to look after. Like many of us, I had become too busy.

I soon realized that being busy meant that *I was always in a hurry*. Memories of my experiment with the dictum of Aristotle came back to me, especially the inner "taste" of being in a hurry. Judging by that "taste," almost the whole of my life was being lived in a hurry. When I was speaking to someone, I was inwardly in a hurry to have him finish so I could speak; when I was hurt by someone or resentful, I saw, by the "taste" of it, that my emotions were *in a hurry* to have their satisfaction, if not in action, then in thought.

Perhaps it was an obvious truth, but it only gradually became clear to me that being in a hurry had to do with my relationship to my mind and that the outer expression in how I moved and acted was only a result of my inner condition, as was the continuous muscular tension in my neck, back and shoulders—and elsewhere. If I was too busy, it was because I was a plaything of the thoughts and images that automatically came in and out of my mind without my "permission."

But it was possible at any given moment to become free of this puppetlike submission to the endless chain of thoughts and images that steal our time from us. It was not so much a matter of organizing one's activities, but of what the early Christians called "guarding the mind."

These thoughts and images in endless procession steal our time because they steal our attention. We give them more attention than is necessary—in this consists the essence of our helplessness in front of all the demands that life makes upon us and all the opportunities (or temptations) that it offers us. What is necessary, so the ancient wisdom advises us, is to confirm for ourselves that we have the power not to be swallowed by our thoughts.

This will not be easy. Our culture, since the age of the Enlightenment, has tended to consider thought the highest principle of the mind—and so it is, no doubt, but only when it is the kind of thought that emerges from the whole being, the kind of vision and mentation that is a property of the Self. What we experience as thought when our minds are on automatic is worlds apart from the intelligence that resides in the Self.

Like the warrior Arjuna, we are called to free ourselves from our attraction to all the emotions and views—symbolized as the "teachers and kinsmen" with whom we have grown up—which have shaped our lives. We are called to free our mind, our attention, from its absorption in its own automatic functioning. We are called to "fight," to step back in ourselves and allow the entrance of something that is incomprehensible to the ego-driven mind. This incomprehensible "something" is not the plaything of time.

In its practical expressions, the ancient wisdom speaks to us of the steps and degrees by which a man or woman can become progressively open to the reality and action of the Self. No doubt it would be foolish to imagine that in our ordinary, everyday lives we can easily cultivate the kind of receptivity toward the Self that is portrayed for us in the lives of the masters and pupils of the great traditions. But even the very first steps in this direction, guided by the ideas that wisdom has injected into the

stream of our culture, can help heal our painful relationship to time.

To those of us who are too busy, the very least thing
that wisdom tells us is that we can step back, not so much
from our activities, but from our thoughts. When we try
this we may find a hint of the next step that we can take.
In that space that appears when we try to see our
thoughts instead of letting them frighten us or goad us,
we may sense that our living body is there asking for our
calm attention. No man or woman can be too busy when
there is even the beginning of a calm relationship
between the mind and the body. When the mind and
body quietly move toward each other, a man or woman
begins to become a grownup. And, whatever it may mean
to be a wise man or woman, surely the first step is to
become a grownup. A grown-up man or woman may have
to move very fast and do many things, but he or she is
never in a hurry. Ah, so that is what Aristotle meant!

THE FEAR OF THE FUTURE
AND THE HABIT OF WORRYING

The strange story of Kirzai may be taken as a message to
us from the ancient wisdom about the normal relationship to our own individual future. The young Kirzai sac-
rifices his immediate gain to help a man whom he does
not consciously recognize, but who in fact is himself
grown old. "The desert will repay you," says the old Kirzai
after drinking the water given to him by his younger self

and then mounting his camel. It is all he can say and all he needs to say.

The desert will repay you: it is these words and their many-layered meaning that we can bring to the second aspect of our contemporary pathology of time—the habit of worrying. Find a man or woman who is too busy and you are certain to find an individual who always worries. Yet, as we shall see, from the most ancient times wisdom has been trying to teach mankind that the future obeys laws that are far different than we can imagine. When we worry, we are assuming we know what is likely to happen in the future and our emotions are employing thought in order to deal in imagination with this presumed future before it happens.

But what does it really mean to plan to attend to the future, to provide for what we can rightfully assume is going to come to us with the passage of time? This is an immense question, a question that can connect our everyday recurrent anxieties with the great scale of human life in its relationship to the cosmos. What is the relationship between our individual lives and the life of mankind itself, the earth and nature? If we are on earth for a purpose, that purpose has to do with what the future will bring or can bring. What then is the relationship between my and your individual future and the future of mankind?

If we observe ourselves when we are worrying, we may see that what we feel is strongly akin to the profound sense of loneliness that afflicts so many of us in our modern culture. When I worry, I feel cut off from my life—and this sense of being cut off from life is practically a definition of loneliness. It is quite different when we are confronting genuine dangers and genuine possibilities—that is, possibilities that reflect reality and the real world. Fear of genuine, possible danger, from either nature or people, is never a waste of time or energy. On the contrary, such fear engages us in the world of real forces, a world in which we may be defeated but never isolated. "Fear" and "sorrow" are words reflecting man's painful but meaningful encounter with the real world; anxiety and nervousness reflect our capture by a meaningless imaginary reality invented by the mind in service to the revolving automatisms of emotional reaction. In the state of worrying, there is no such thing as *thinking* in the fully human sense. In this state, thought, which is meant to inform us about the real world, becomes instead a puppet of the emotional reactions.

At this point the ancient wisdom advises us to develop in ourselves an instrument for real thinking and vision, the instrument of the mind, for which man was created. The future simply cannot be seen with the egoistic or anxious mind. We are on earth to do things that only human beings can do, but none of them can be done until we are able to think as a grown-up man or woman thinks. Worrying is not thinking.

From the teachings of wisdom we learn that the fundamental aims of human life can be attained only alongside the search to have Self in one's presense. The story of Kirzai is a partial hint that this search has powerful implications for our own individual future well-being. The full idea is that reality, or—if one wishes—*God,* provides only for the individual who is struggling for the Self at the same time that he is carrying out the necessary obligations of outer life. To care for one's Self, to attend to the Self, is to open oneself to the influence of the great and beneficent laws and forces that created man as man—a being made, as is said, "in the image of God." To care for the Self is to find a real future. To care only for the everyday obligations of life, or to care in a wrong way for them, is to be abandoned by the greatness of nature, to be abandoned by the future. *The desert will repay you:* that is, die to your illusory values and the search for your Self will bring you what you need now and in the future. Otherwise you will perish as a lonely human being, however crowded with things and people and events your life may be as a merely human animal.

The old Middle Eastern aphorism, "Trust in Allah, but tie your camel first," should not be taken too lightly. The question is, how much and what *kind* of attention to give to the needs and demands of our lives? In the search for the inner Self, what kind of care are we obliged to give to our outer lives, our material needs and desires, our families, our loves, our health, our work and calling, our normal desires to be of help to others and to build something, discover something, create something—or even just to get by, but with honor and self-respect? Certainly, if we give too little attention to the outer aspect of our lives, sooner or later it will take *all* our attention; we will have no time or means to follow the great search. If we plan too little for our health or material security, for example, eventually problems of health or money will overtake us and stand in the way of pursuing truth; we will be forced to spend all our time on them, like the animals in the Buddhist symbology of the lower worlds who are compelled to spend all their time hunting for food or fighting off danger.

But, on the other hand, if we care "too much," if we care in a wrong way about our outer life—if we are continually possessed by worry—we are equally in danger of losing the time allotted to man for the purpose of searching for the Self. To be possessed by worry is a kind of denial—in the sense that the man or woman possessed by the habit of worry can have no intimation and can never verify that the greatness of nature requires developing human beings and will provide for them. This is the real meaning of the ancient idea of providence.

In the gospel of Matthew, Jesus tells his disciples:

> Therefore I say unto you, Take no thought for your life, what ye shall eat, or what ye shall drink; nor yet for your body; what ye shall put on. Is not the life more than meat, and the body more than raiment?[7]

Jesus is not telling the disciples to ignore the outer aspect of life. He is telling them not to be taken by worrying about it. The Greek verb *merimnan*, translated here as "taking thought," is best rendered in this passage as *to be anxious about.* John Wyclif (fourteenth century) translated it as "be not busy to your life." Other translations are equally clear: "I charge you not to be *over-anxious* about your lives" (Weymouth); "Do not *trouble* about what you are to eat and drink" (Moffatt); and, in some recent versions, "I bid you not to *fret* about your life" (Rieu) and "do not be *anxious* about your life" (RSV). As in all the sayings of Jesus, what is at issue goes far beyond psychotherapeutic comfort. It is the whole meaning and direction of life and the future that is at stake.

The words of Jesus that follow point to the idea that there is a specific kind of future reserved for man, considered as a unique inhabitant of the earth. But to enter into this future a man or woman must give attention, or care, to that for which man is uniquely created: the Self within and above, what is spoken of here and elsewhere as the "kingdom of God."

Man occupies a specific place in nature:

> Behold the fowls of the air; for they sow not, neither do they reap, nor gather into barns; yet your heavenly Father feedeth them. Are ye not much better than they? . . . And why take ye thought for raiment? Consider the lilies of the field, how they grow; they toil not, neither do they spin. . . . Wherefore, if God so clothe the grass of the field, which today is, and tomorrow is cast into the oven, shall he not much more clothe you, O ye of little faith? [8]

What is man? What are we made for? What kind of future is calling to us? And what can we do to prepare for that future?

> Therefore take no thought, saying, What shall we eat? or, What shall we drink? or, Wherewithal shall we be clothed? . . . for your heavenly Father knoweth that ye have need of all these things. *But seek ye first the kingdom of God,* and his righteousness; and all these things shall be added unto you. Take therefore no thought for the morrow; for the morrow shall take thought for the things of itself. Sufficient unto the day is the evil thereof.[9]

Seek ye first the kingdom of God: words that have entered the blood and bone of countless millions of men and women. But how to understand what they mean? As with all the great words of wisdom, there is no one single meaning to them. But this particular passage is surely telling us, among many other things, that a man or woman must give *first priority* to what transcends the outer needs and desires of our existence—and these outer needs and desires are by no means trivial or narrowly materialistic. This outer world includes the people we love, the children for whom we are responsible, the work and the activity that make up our day, the challenges to think and know and create and serve that call us to science, scholarship, art, music, business, medicine, law and even war. What could possibly be more fundamental than everything, *everything* that we love and hate and desire and want, everything that engages us, terrifies us, bores us, draws us in; everything that the world and human culture create for us and offer us; what could have greater priority than our health and well-being, our body that communicates and demands things from us with its overmastering pleasures and pain and the thoughts that serve these pleasures and these pains? What is more important even than what we *imagine to be* God, what we *think* is good and evil, what we *take to be* duty and obligation, what we *view* as service to others? Again, what is greater than—*everything?*

"Your words have no meaning," says Tat to Hermes.

"I will not fight," says Arjuna to Krishna.

Perhaps now we begin to glimpse what it *feels* like *not to be able to grasp in thought* what it means to remember the Self. All the great masters of wisdom speak against the habit of trying to explain the inner search. The Buddhists tell us to forgo our explanations, the Christians tell us to have faith, the Jews tell us only to trust, the Moslems to submit, the Hindus to let go, yet all these wise directions against the habit of thinking too much about ultimate things, all this wise advice itself falls into our isolated intellects and becomes once again mere fodder for the head that is always pretending it is who we are. And it often gets translated even into methods of defeating the tyranny of time. Psychological methods, philosophical methods, religious exercises.

And all of these exercises work for a time. For a precious little time. They all work, they all can help us get over a rough patch, ease the mind for a while, give a little breather. But then, rather soon, something closes over them like water closing over a stone or over a massive object slowly but inevitably sinking.

Time is stronger than any exercise, than any words. Time remains the great incomprehensible problem of life and thought. When Augustine[10] wrote, "I know well enough what it is, provided that nobody asks me," he was only expressing what every philosopher and every human being realizes when they try to grasp the nature of time. *It cannot be understood!* And yet it is overwhelmingly real! How is it that what is most real is what is most incomprehensible? What does that imply about the limits of what we call thought?

Time is deeper and stronger than anything else in our lives; it take everything with it, nothing is bigger than time, nothing survives its power.

And *therefore:* whatever there may be that can meet time or overcome its tyranny—this, too, will surely be incomprehensible to the mind. How could we ever have expected to meet the depth of time's incomprehensibility with thought or ideas or methods as we usually understand them?

"Fight, Arjuna!"

It is only the Self that overcomes time.

Therefore: everything we think, every method we try, must be rooted in the search to remember the Self, the search we cannot "do," the Self we cannot grasp, the "remembering" that is the mystery of mysteries.

There is a remarkable passage about man's relationship to the future in the writings of Ralph Waldo Emerson. It occurs in his most famous essay, "The Over-Soul." In this early work, first published when he was thirty-seven years old, Emerson announces the great, underlying theme that forms the basis of everything he was to write in his long, prodigiously productive life. The idea of the Over-Soul is that the universe, the greatness of nature, is everywhere penetrated by an invisible, conscious Selfhood upon which it, nature, depends. The greatness of nature is this Selfhood in its manifestation. The uniqueness of man is that he is given the possibility and the duty consciously to attend to this Selfhood, this *soul*, within himself, and to sense throughout his life that this soul *is* himself. "Man," writes Emerson, "is a stream whose source is hidden. Our being is descending into us from we know not whence." Then, speaking of man's relationship to time, he goes on:

> The Supreme Critic on the errors of the past and the present, and the only prophet of that which must be, is that great nature in which we rest, as the earth lies in the soft arms of the atmosphere; that Unity, that Over-Soul, within which every man's particular being is contained and made one with all other. . . . We live in succession, in division, in parts, in particles. Meantime within man is the soul of the whole; the wise silence . . . to which every part and particle is related; the eternal ONE. . . .[11]

And now, speaking specifically of man's relationship to the future, Emerson offers an extraordinary vision of what it means that the future is unknown to us—what this obvious fact means and what this intrinsic unknowability of the future calls on us to search for within ourselves. In what Emerson writes, we shall see the astonishing idea that the future is unknown in the same sense that the Self is unknown! *To remember is the same mystery as to foretell!* What we are to be is the same thing at that which we have always been—in our depths.

TIME AND THE SOUL

Once again, let us go slowly. The soul speaks to man in rare and great moments of our lives, and this communication of the soul (which is the same as the Over-Soul of the world) Emerson calls *revelation.* Such communications, says Emerson, "are always attended by the emotion of the sublime. For this communication is an influx of the Divine mind into our own mind." The depth and duration of this experience vary, depending, as Emerson tells us, upon the state of the individual. But, he says, whatever the depth or degree of this contact with the Self (or soul), it is intrinsically incomprehensible to the ordinary time-driven mind—except when it actually is taking place. In these moments when the contact is actually taking place, the mind submits. The mind becomes quiet. It accepts. It obeys. *But it does not understand*—in the way it always tries to understand. In such moments one sees that what the mind is reaching for cannot be attained by the mind, but only by its submission to another force. In this submission, which takes place instantly and gently in the moment of contact, time is overcome.

Slowly. The descent of the Self into our ordinary self appears as both an overmastering truth and an incomprehensible, inexplicable reality. Like Tat standing before Heremes, like Arjuna before Krishna, we cannot grasp the truth that so exquisitely draws us toward itself. Does this condition of the pupil before the master, of the ordinary self before the great Self, offer us the answer to the great riddle of time? Emerson's answer is a resounding yes.

He reminds us that the men and women of history who have manifested this contact with the Self have experienced it in themselves and have often been regarded by others as touched by "insanity," a term that Tat uses to describe what the guidance of his teacher is evoking in him.

Emerson provides an intriguing perspective on this incomprehensibility of the soul's communications. No one who is at all interested in what is called mysticism or higher states of consciousness can afford to ignore his formulations on this point. "The nature of these revelations is the same," he says. "They do not answer the question which the understanding asks. *The soul answers never by words, but by the thing itself that is inquired after.*"

The answer to the question of time, the soul's answer to the question of time, is not anything in words or ideas.

Time is incomprehensible to the mind that asks about it, *our* mind. *The soul's answer to the problem of time is the experience of timeless being.* There is no other answer.

What, then, specifically of time and the future? Emerson now begins by telling us, "Revelation is the disclosure of the soul." And then he warns us against the obsessive desire to predict the future, trying to prepare in an anxious way for something that transcends not just our present date and time of existence but our present state of consciousness. The unknowability of the future is like the wing of a great being that is the Self in all its unknownness.

> The popular notion of revelation is that it is a telling of for-
> tunes. . . . [The] understanding seeks to find answers to
> sensual questions, and undertakes to tell from God how
> long men shall exist, what their hands shall do, and who
> shall be their company, adding names, and dates, and
> places. But we must pick no locks. We must check this
> low curiosity. An answer in words is delusive; it is really
> no answer to the questions you ask. *Do not require a
> description of the countries toward which you sail. The
> description does not describe them to you, and tomorrow you
> arrive there, and know them by inhabiting them.*

Do not imagine, says Emerson, that the great masters of wisdom offer to answer questions about the future in the way these questions are usually asked. What Emerson now writes should perhaps be committed to memory by every man or woman driven by anxious worry concerning his or her future well-being:

> These questions which we lust to ask about the future are a confession of sin. *God has no answer for them.* No answer in words can reply to a question of things. It is not in an arbitrary "decree of God," but in the nature of man, that a veil shuts down on the facts of tomorrow; for the soul will not have us read any other cipher than that of cause and effect. *By this veil, which curtains events, it instructs the children of men to live in to-day.*

He continues:

> The only mode of obtaining an answer to these questions of the senses is to forgo all low curiosity, and, accepting the tide of being which floats us into the secret of nature, work and live, and all unawares the advancing soul has built and forged for itself a new condition, and the question and the answer are one.

CHAPTER 7

A MODEST EXERCISE

Here is something to try. It may or may not be of help to everyone. Its sole purpose is to provide the mind with a quieter space within which we may find a first approach to the search for the Self. There are many such first approaches. I have found this modest exercise of help in verifying, actually witnessing, how the habit of worrying wastes the attention and therefore the time needed for finding one's inner life. Practiced with some degree of diligence and relaxation, and with some advance guidance, it can also show us that there is in each of us a natural attraction of the attention toward another sense of time and the Self. *This natural attraction toward the Self is an important part of that which our ordinary mind cannot comprehend.*

One word of warning: it is only an exercise, an experiment, something to try for a little while and then let go.

However, although it is only a modest exercise, it echoes some powerful metaphysical ideas—namely, the idea, the strangest of all ideas about time, that everything that happens to us in this life has all happened before, and not only once but many times. This idea of *recurrence* may be found in the myths and philosophies of numerous traditions—in India, in the teachings of Plato and in many other doctrines throughout the world. It was of great interest to Nietzsche and was developed with considerable power in the writings of P. D. Ouspensky.[12] In other forms, we encounter the experiential equivalent of this idea in the doctrine of destiny and fate as it is expressed throughout the Middle East and in Teutonic legend. The future already exists; your life has already been lived; you have only to inhabit this life as it "unreels"—inhabit it from moment to moment with faith in the Creator of all lives. This moment-to-moment faith in the Creator of destiny is the experiential equivalent of the moment-to-moment search for contact with one's Self.

Taken by itself, the idea of recurrence or destiny seems at first to do away with the normal human experience of free will and choice. As such, it is unacceptable to most of us. Every day, every hour, sometimes even every minute of our lives, we are faced with choices and decisions about great or small things. The idea of recurrence and destiny seems to make human life too passive, too accepting in a weak and ignoble way.

Yet wherever the idea of destiny is seriously offered, it is accompanied by promptings involving choice and struggle. It is a complete misunderstanding to think of this idea as urging a weak passivity. The teachings of wisdom never lead us away from the active principle in human nature. On the contrary, always and in everything, wisdom calls us to *choose,* to decide, to sacrifice, but always with an intensive, active attention. It is a serious misunderstanding ever to read the great metaphysical traditions as counsels of passivity. But is this not a blatant contradiction? How can one entertain the idea of recurrence and destiny and still hold to the idea of free will?

No authentic expression of the idea of destiny ever seeks to mitigate this contradiction. On the contrary, it flings the contradiction in our faces. The logical mind recoils and rejects one or another side of the contradiction. It would seem impossible to hold on to destiny and freedom at one and the same time. It is here that the guidance of wisdom begins to "bite"—here is a place where we see that these ancient doctrines are not intended as easy consolations or mere explanations. Behind this contradiction, invisible to the intellect in its ordinary state, there lies the deep resolution of this contradiction, the great meaning of the idea of recurrence and destiny. But it cannot be given in words. It can only be given in experience.

Eliot cannot understand what Max is demanding of him through the word "Remember." And so he is sent back in time to witness the life that has already been lived.

There *is* a great harmonious resolution of this paradox. Be assured of that. Eliot is sent back in time not only to witness his life, but eventually, through the deepening of this witnessing, to *will* his life. Behind the contradiction between destiny and freedom there lies yet another contradiction, yet another reality impossible to explain. Behind the contradiction between destiny and freedom there lies the paradox that man is called to will the life that he has not "chosen," the life that he is given. We are speaking now of something that is not only unknown to the mind but also unknown to the emotional side of our nature. And what is unknown to the emotions is often anticipated through the perceptions of fear and dread. The deeper meaning of the idea of destiny and recurrence invites us to fight against that fear and to search instead for a feeling that is beyond preference, beyond wanting or desiring or wishing or liking.

"Fight, Arjuna!"

The exercise is simply this: during the day, as you enter into one or another situation of your life, try to look upon it in advance as having already happened. Look upon every detail as predetermined. Try sometime to treat your life like a script that has already been written, as a play in which you are only an actor rehearsing a part. Try to regard the immediate future as already existing. You are like a tiny insect crawling up a tree. The tree exists already, the roots, trunk, branches and leaves are all already there. What you call time is only your movement from the roots to the branches that are already there. The insect imagines that the branches and the leaves are appearing out of nonexistence, but it is not so. The branches and leaves are there, waiting. Try to look at your life in this way—for a day, for an hour, even for a minute.

Forget about whether or not it is actually true that the future already exists. This is an exercise, nothing more, something to do with your thought, your attitude, your attention. Try it first with small external things, the meal you prepare, say, or the telephone call you are about to make. Is the toast burned? It was already burned beforehand. Do you dial a wrong number and get an irritated stranger on the line? It had already happened before you "did" it and the stranger's irritation with it.

In this most external stage of the exercise, there is an element of play and amusement, but along with the amusement one very soon feels something of quite another quality. It is best not to try immediately to give this new quality a name, but just to note that something is being liberated in a subtle and gentle way. It is best just to note, without naming, the possibility of a faint sense of welcoming, as though there are parts of one's self that are like parts of one's family, family that one has never known. . . . Just note the sense of welcoming. That impression is the most important thing at this stage of the exercise, a welcoming that is calm and tinted with a subtle sense of gladness.

It is a question not to be answered, but only felt: what is being given up in this exercise? And what, in consequence, is showing itself?

But the exercise needs to develop further. The next stage is to look to one's *own* behavior in this way. Take one or another situation and, as you enter into it, try to regard everything you do or say—all your outer behavior—as already there beforehand, as predetermined. Did you do something clumsy, knock something over? The event was there before it happened. Did you say something foolish, did you betray a secret, make an unintended promise? Your saying it was already there before you actually did it. Keep the exercise to small things, the details of life. It is in the small things that life is lived, in any case. The big things—apart from birth and death—are actually made up *entirely* of small things. But that is another subject.

This part of the exercise is more difficult than the first part. Even more than the first part of the exercise, it is almost impossible to remember to try it, or, if one remembers it, to actually try it; or, if one actually tries it, to sustain it for more than a few seconds. But it *is* possible. And again, it will show us something fairly astonishing about how our relationship to time is involved with our false beliefs about ourselves. Where the ancient wisdom tells us time is illusory, it is telling us that we are immersed in illusions about ourselves—our identity, our powers, our freedom. If you try to grasp the ancient teachings about time without seeing what they are saying about your own self, you will never begin to understand the real meaning of these ideas. When the wise speak of the mirage of time, they are speaking of the mirage of our self.

But there, in the desert, it is no mirage: there, with nothing else but the pitiless truth beating down upon us, we see what time will do to us. We must take an action that is for our selves, freeing ourselves, like Kirzai, from our attachments to the illusory values of the world of unnecessary things and events. What we identify ourselves with—our physical body, our automatic emotional reactions and socially conditioned obsessions, our slavery to a mind that keeps repeating mechanical patterns of explanation and manipulation—all this has to be seen through. There, before me, is myself grown old and about to die.

If we treat our behavior as predetermined—if we do this as an *exercise*—it means temporarily surrendering our sense of agency, of "free will." It means entertaining the idea that nothing of what we say or do comes from our own, inner Self. It is that Self that is free and conscious, and if we entertain the idea that all that we ordinarily do is predetermined, it means entertaining the idea that our Self is not yet there, acting in our lives, not yet there, speaking in our lives. To consider this thought, and to actually experiment with it in one's life, is to approach the feeling that the search for the Self is necessary. There, under the "pitiless" sun of truth, only the Self can live, and only the search for the Self is supported. "The desert will repay you."

This second stage of the exercise can help us to take much more seriously the idea that we are asleep to the existence of the Self within us. All the paths of wisdom lead across this idea; and the actual practices that the ancient teachings have offered mankind throughout the ages lead an individual to the concrete experience of this idea. What we are speaking of here as an exercise is meant only to dramatize the reality of the idea; the full experience itself obviously demands another kind of guidance.

Concerning the ancient teachings about time, however, we need to repeat: what is said about time in the wisdom traditions of the world cannot be separated from the teachings about the Self. If we make the mistake of separating these two, if we limit our interest to the philosophical question of time without also attending to the question of the truth about ourselves, we will never be able to receive the help offered by these great teachings and philosophies. We will make the question of time into what is only an intriguing intellectual puzzle or material for science fiction or grist for ingenious but humanly irrelevant scientific speculations about the origins and destiny of the so-called universe.

This second stage of the exercise—that is, regarding one's own words and behavior as predetermined—can provide a glimpse of a capacity within ourselves whose importance it is impossible to overestimate. Specifically, this is the capacity to allow our words and actions to proceed without identifying ourselves with them. It is only a glimpse, but a vitally necessary glimpse, of the intrinsically human power *to step back* not only from outer events but from our own actions. This capacity, this power to step back from our own behavior, is never supported or recognized in our culture. Our culture does not know about it or value it. Everything in our world pushes us to ignore this capacity. What we call commitment, passion, "love," ambition, devotion, care, concern, pleasure—all these almost always involve our being devoured by the objects of our emotions. We are conditioned to feel that we cannot really care for someone or something unless we are obsessed. But the study of the lives of inwardly developed men and women shows us that the capacity to step back from one's own behavior allows an individual to be more, not less, caring and loving and devoted.

Why this is so may be understood through considering the third and most difficult stage of this exercise—namely, to regard one's *inner reactions* as predetermined, as already there. This is the most "inner" stage of the exercise. It is not a matter of events that happen to us, or of our actions and words; it is a matter of what reactions take place within ourselves. Could it be that they, too, are included in the idea of recurrence and destiny?

To try this part of the exercise is to search for an aspect of the mind that can separate itself not only from what one says or does but from what one ordinarily thinks and feels in the usual situations of life. Is there a part of the mind that is actually independent of our thoughts and reactions?

We know that the answer is yes. We know from experience that there are moments in life—moments of great crisis, perhaps, or sorrow, or wonder, or even terror, or shock, or tenderness—in which a conscious attention appears within ourselves that is independent of our emotions, thoughts and sensations. It is an attention that is pure presence. It sees what is, what is taking place within ourselves. It sees what thoughts are proceeding, what emotional reactions are being activated, what physical sensations and impulses are being triggered. The appearance of this conscious attention brings with it a new sense of *I am,* I exist. I exist here, I exist now. It is not itself a thought or emotion or sensation. Or, perhaps, it is more accurate to say that it is all of these together, but related together in such a way as to conduct an entirely new capacity of conscious presence. And, invariably, it brings with it *a completely new sense of time.*

Time stops. We move, it seems, in slow motion. We may be in a situation that demands instant action, or a battery of complex movements may be needed, perhaps, to save one's life. A second is like an hour. And through it all, an attention exists that is intensely calm, intensely present and alert, intensely *interested.* The body? The body obeys this new attention without the slightest resistance. The emotions? They are there, but they do not interfere. They quiet down and eventually retreat. The mind, the thoughts? They no longer race uncontrollably through my awareness, they no longer distract me. On the contrary, suddenly, my mind, like my body, becomes an obedient servant. My thoughts now collect together in relevant associations and the mind begins to do its proper work of thinking to some purpose, of serving a great intention. *Time has stopped*—or, one might say, a completely new dimension of time has appeared, the time of another self, another dimension, a higher reality. This quality of time is an aspect of what the great teachings call *eternity*. Or they may call it immortality. Or, simply, *life, long life.*

Such experiences are common in cases of sudden physical danger when lives may depend on instant action. But they are often given to us also in moments of great emotional shock—as in the encounter with the death of a loved one, or an immense disappointment or betrayal, or in moments of unexpected triumph and good fortune, or in moments when one is suddenly in a strange new place, or suddenly encountering a wonder of nature, or in the intensity of passion. . . . We know such moments. We cannot deny that there exists within us the possibility of another quality of conscious attention. But we do not have the intellectual tools by which to evaluate these moments and see what they are connected to and to what kind of struggle they invite us. In fact, as the wisdom teachings tell us, such experiences are glimpses of the Self. Or, should we say, glimpses *by* the Self, that is, moments when the person we ordinarily are feels him- or herself as seen and known by another conscious presence which is, paradoxically, also one's own real self, one's own intimate identity. An identity that we have all but forgotten existed within us, waiting for us, calling to us.

We know such moments exist. And therefore we know, even if we do not remember, that we are not the self we think we are. We know, even if we do not remember, that time as we ordinarily experience it is not what it seems. In such moments a witness has appeared within us—and it is we who are being witnessed. The seer, the witness, is also *myself.*

Who, then, *am* I?

The modest exercise of treating one's own psyche as predetermined in time does not pretend to bring such exalted glimpses of the true Self within. It has a much more limited purpose: to acquaint us with the mind's ability to step back from itself and to offer evidence, however fleeting, that this capacity opens us to a greater engagement with life and not, as might have been expected, a withdrawal from life. *To show us that time rushes by because we are not engaged enough in life.* Not enough of our being is involved in our own life. To be devoured by our life is not to be engaged in living. On the contrary, when we are devoured by life it means the Self, one's own Self, is not present.

This stepping back is something the mind wants to do: we need to note that fact, which we verify during exercises such as this. The mind: by this is meant a kind of conscious attention that is profoundly and breathtakingly intimate, that knows and feels itself, as I, *myself,* and not as the self I have been conditioned to identify with. This mind yearns to step back and exist purely and simply.

This is a desire of the mind, a true passion of the mind. Just as the body has its desires and needs, just as our root emotions drive us naturally toward love and affection, just as the intellectual powers desire, naturally, to gather all our experience and information under the rubric of natural concepts and ideas—just as these three main parts of ourselves have these natural desires, so too does the mind, the psyche of the whole human being, have its own desires. The mind, the psyche, the seat of attention—this mind yearns simply to be. *Our mind yearns to step back from our lives.* And in stepping back it can then consciously enter into much more of life, the life of the universe itself and, within that universe, once again enter into the details of our human condition on earth. Wisdom tells us that we are not meant to live only as animals with complicated brains, as "talking animals." We are built to be like gods inhabiting the life of earth, just as, individually, we are meant to ensoul our own bodies and our own relationships during the years allotted to us.

CHAPTER 8

THE OTHER DOOR

No matter what we say or think, no matter what we do, what we try, time is passing. We will grow old, we will die. If we live long enough to experience the process of growing old, we will very likely begin to look very differently at the things we desired most, the goals that seemed so important when we were younger. This is obvious in the case of desires that depend on biological age, but it is also true, and perhaps much more important, with respect to things that have nothing to do with the biological condition of our bodies. The goals of fame, wealth and power, for example, which are not necessarily biologically determined, look very different when death, or—as it has been called—"the other door," becomes more visible.

A younger person who is driven by ambition is one thing; often it may even be admirable, up to a certain point, as an expression of energy. But an older man or woman with the same kind of personal ambition evokes pity in us or even fear. A younger person accumulating money or material goods, establishing his or her personal identity in a career or business, is one thing. An older person ardently driven in the same way seems to be foolish. And so it is with many of the things we crave and seek in our lives. As death gradually becomes more visible, more real, as the passage of time is felt in its metaphysical significance, our perception of every person, every object and every situation in our lives begins to change—at least for some of us and at some moments.

People differ greatly, at least on the surface, in the way they regard the inevitable approach of death, but when anyone thinks seriously about death, in that moment everything in life looks different. In that kind of thinking, where the fact of death influences how we regard the people and things that make up our lives—in that moment, our attitude toward ourselves and our lives and the world we live in begins to converge with what the traditions of wisdom have always taught about time and reality.

THE ART OF PONDERING

Certain forms of Buddhism and Hinduism, for example, speak of the unreality or illusoriness of the world and of our personal identity. Ordinarily, such an idea may seem fanciful or exaggerated. But when we are looking at death it does not seem so fanciful. If we consider ourselves, if we consider the infinite stretches of time that

preceded our birth and the infinite stretches of time that
will follow our death, if we ponder the fact that we have
arisen and will return to an endlessly vast sea of nonexistence, then we may feel the intrinsic insignificance of
what we are and what we do in the life we have lived.
And if it is true for us, it is also true for everyone we see
or know, for everyone we have heard of and for every
thing, every living thing, every inanimate thing, including the earth itself and the sun and the stars above us. It
is all, we may come to feel, composed basically of the
nothingness; it is all a momentary, insubstantial shudder
in the ocean of nonexistence.

Only note: such thoughts do not necessarily make us
sad. Not necessarily. True, they *may* be the expression or
the cause of anguish or a sense of futility. But not necessarily. Try holding such a thought for a longer time and
see if your emotional associations don't rather calm down
and themselves return to some place of relative nonexistence. Just note what can take place by holding thoughts
like this and patiently allowing their weight to be felt. It
may be surprising to discover that a certain feeling
appears that is not sadness at all, or, properly speaking,
resignation. Don't let go of the thought; return to it again
and again, trying to let it act. Note what takes place in the
mind. Such a process in relation to thoughts of this kind
has a definite name: it is called *pondering*. It is a completely lost art in our culture, an art we must rediscover in
order to let the questions about time and aging and death
have a beneficent action upon us. For in that pondering a

certain new quality of the mind can begin to appear, an entirely new quality of thought. We may consider this kind of thought in a rather startling way: is it a *glimpse of how the Self thinks when it exists in us?*

IMMORTALITY AND THE OCEAN
OF NONEXISTENCE

But what of the idea of the immortality of soul that in one or another form lies at the heart of our Western spiritual traditions and that has brought hope and solace to so many millions? How does this idea stand alongside the intimation of the insubstantiality of our lives in the ocean of endless time? Don't the two ideas contradict each other?

In fact, there is no contradiction. The immortality spoken of in the wisdom teachings of the West refers to the existence of the soul outside of time as we know it. It does not refer to the continuation of the social self for endless years and ages of days and nights and hours and minutes. The wisdom of the West points us to existence in *eternity.* Eternity is not at all the same thing as endless duration.

But this again is not a problem to be intellectually solved, it is a matter for pondering. And pondering in this case may begin in a rather different way than with the idea of endless time, endless nonexistence before and after one's life. For many of us, the idea of the soul and its immortality begins in early childhood with a wordless, powerful sense that there is something in ourselves which is our true, intimate identity and which only we can know, which no one else sees. It is an identity that exists between oneself and God. As a child, one may say "my soul" and mean by that one's intimate existence, one's consciousness—independent of being this or that parent's child, this or that sex, this or that race, this or that quality or strength or weakness, talent, beauty, wealth or poverty, health or illness. To oneself as a child, the soul is the independent sense of I, *I am,* not in words, but definite, powerful, unmistakable.

This is one element in the idea of the soul that needs to enter into our pondering. But there are other elements that are necessary in order to allow this idea to have its full action in us.

As we grow older, we identify ourselves with how our external world—family, friends, other people, the culture at large—regards us. More and more my identity and name come to mean something else, something other than the independent sense of *I am* that I touched so often as a young child. More and more I am now identified with just those conditions which other people *can* see and know or which are put into me by external influences, and this includes our thoughts and opinions, which come to us from outside, and many of our emotions, our likes and dislikes, our ideals and values, our sense of self-respect and place. And more and more we identify ourselves with our bodies, with their pleasures and pains and the changes that take place in them, including, of course, the intensity of sexual awakening and sensation and all the emotions that are attached to sexuality. We identify ourselves with our social class or ethnic group or gender or nationality or any one or more of a hundred such aspects of our communal life.

And now the word "soul"—or its equivalent—begins to mean very many different things. Sometimes it means only the mind in its ordinary condition, composed, as it is, of notions and thoughts and views which have been put into me from outside or which have accidentally flown into my mind and have taken up residence there, along with the "proofs" and justifications which these errant notions proudly bear as their proper plumage. Can such entities as these vagabond thoughts and arguments be identified as my self, my soul? It is enough only to go "back in time" and remember oneself as a small child to see that our ordinary thoughts are not our *self*. It is only enough to remember how we confronted ultimate reality as children—the reality of death and injury—to see that our everyday thoughts, even our careful, logical thinking, are not the self, not the soul. When the young child *needs* to understand, when you or I need to understand a mystery, an ultimate fact, an overpowering reality, then and only then do we taste the beginning of a new kind of thinking that comes from the inner self. Such thinking has very little in common with the views and opinions that fly in and out of the socially conditioned mind.

So our thoughts are not the soul.

What, then, of our emotions? Surely, whatever the soul may be, it has to do with feeling, deep, intimate feeling. But can violent emotions such as anger, fear or craving be called "intimate"? Are they "deep"? Or are they only over-powering? Where do they come from? There is an answer to this question, but it is a hard answer to accept.

These powerful emotions that continually sweep over us as we grow up and develop into adults are strangely unconnected to the deep, intimate sense of *I am* that we knew as children, and that more and more rarely breaks through into our awareness. Yet all human beings, every man or woman, must, by some unknown law of nature, be a *self*. As beings created for consciousness, created as reflectors of the Original Consciousness itself, all men and women must be and live as *selves,* not as merely bio-logically sensitive creations. It is as though we are com-manded, condemned perhaps, to affirm ourselves as self-conscious beings who exist. And a self-conscious being, of its very nature, is not and cannot accept to be the slave of passing time. *No self can die! Every self seeks to live without destruction by time.*

It is a matter to be pondered. Those aspects of our-selves that take the place of the intimate sense of *I am* that we touch as children—those aspects that take its place are just those emotions that are sown into us by a mysteriously damaged cultural and social environment that the traditions of wisdom call, simply, the "world." And these emotional patterns, which may often contain elements of the power of real feelings, but which are dominantly composed of uncontrolled biological forces (as modern psychiatry has seen with great clarity)—*these emotional patterns masquerade as the self.*

THE GREAT WOUND

The intimate childhood sense of *I am* has not been supported, has not been allowed to develop in relation to the
body and the mind that are growing. The true seed of
human immortality, that in a man or woman which really
can resist time, has been driven back as we grew up. It is
a thousand times more vivid and intense than our usual
emotions and it suffers with strange and unbearable
power when it is—when *I* am—given to live on lies and
violence. The essential substance of human selfhood lives
and grows through the experiences of truth. That is its
food. But in the mysteriously and awesomely damaged
world of human society, as we know it, truth is not offered
in any digestible form to the growing child. Something
quite the opposite is offered and, in countless forms, the
intimate sense of self is compelled to retreat into a "subconsciousness" that is unknown to modern psychology. It
is a subconsciousness that is higher than the ordinary self,
not lower; the subconsciousness of finer perception as
opposed to the subconsciousness of repressed biological
need. This "metaphysical repression" is the great wound
shared by every man and woman born into the "world."

The powerful emotions that masquerade as the self
actually protect this metaphysical wound. They affirm
themselves as *I,* but they are not the *I am* within. They
feel like oneself, they are not one's *Self.* And thus, in the
course of our lives a whole structure is formed that acts
like the Self but is not the Self. Were these emotional
"selves" to be removed, the wounded, intimate soul would

again be driven back in pain and starvation. The great myths and legends of ancient traditions present the picture of the inner self held captive by forces that pretend to be one's self but are not.*

The Western doctrine of the immortality of the soul was never a promise of the continued existence after death of the socially conditioned self. The soul, is not the ego. Taken in one way, this idea brings great comfort and can reconcile our common fear of death. Taken in another way, however, it turns into a soporific lie and even strengthens the grip of those very aspects of ourselves from which we need to free ourselves—namely, our selfish and violent emotions as well as the network, called the ego, that binds them together into a psychological prison. But taken in a third way, the ancient idea of the immortal soul becomes a dynamic idea that opens the mind and heart of the growing child and becomes food for the pondering of the searching adult who feels trapped in time and bewildered by death. We need to look more closely at this third approach to the idea of the soul.

But, first, let us be clear about the two approaches, the first bringing justified comfort to our lives and the second

---

*One of the most widely known of these legends is the story of Robin Hood. The true and beloved king, the soul (King Richard the Lionhearted), is in exile, his place taken by the usurper ego, King John. Robin Hood is the outlaw who steals from the rich and gives to the poor, redistributing the substance and energy of the kingdom (the inner kingdom of the individual human being) and making possible the return of the true self to its rightful place. See also the Jewish legend of Solomon and Asmodeus as recounted in my *Money and the Meaning of Life*.

bringing only self-deception and seduction. The comfort
in the idea of the soul is general—the idea that there is an
immortal principle in man, in myself; there *is* an undying
reality; being human, I do live in eternity. But the comfort of this idea is meant as a call to a new quality of life,
a new quality of struggle, not as a reason to do away with
struggle altogether.

The second approach identifies the eternal in man with
what is only socially conditioned and transitory, the social
self, the personal ego. This personal ego has a definite role
to play in human life; it is necessary, it enables us to live
and function in the world as it is. But this ego is meant to
be a secondary reality in ourselves. It is a creature of time.
It was born in time and it will disappear in time. That is
why the teachings of the East speak of it as unreal, as illusory. By illusion is meant dependent, dependent on more
fundamental forces and realities. The ego exists—every
Buddhist or Hindu knows that. But its existence is not
what we feel it to be—that is the problem. In order to feel,
really know, the secondary nature, the "unreality" of the
ego, we need to feel, know, taste directly the actual reality
of the fundamental Self within us. Only then can we be
sure of what it is that is free of time within ourselves.
Without this actual experience of the Self within us, the
idea of the eternal soul is at best only that, a speculative
idea—and, at worst, it becomes an idea that we merge into
our sense of the socially conditioned ego. And in that case
we mistakenly identify what is secondary in ourselves with
what is primary and, imagining we know what the soul is,

we actually work and live to strengthen the illusion, rather than to free ourselves from it.

THE THIRD APPROACH

Now, the third approach: the real hope, the actual taste of reality. How to look at this, this answer to the problem of time, an answer that reaches out across centuries and millennia from the teachings of wisdom to the harried, time-impoverished lives of modern men and women?

We need to think slowly, to ponder. I look at you, we look at each other. We are human beings. There is a self in there, in here. When we love and value another human being, when we look calmly and attentively at each other, we know, we see that there is something in a man or woman that is not of time. *We know it!* Consciousness is not of time. Time is such a painful mystery partly because, when we take stock of our present awareness, it is inconceivable that this awareness is attached to an entity, an animal, that is born and dies. There is a soul in here, in there—the thoughts and emotions, even though they are attached to an ego, are signs of a soul, signs of an immortal principle, an undying reality. But that which tries to express the soul—the person we are—is the damaged instrument, the prison which we call the ego and which pretends it is not merely the instrument of the true self but the soul itself. The soul, that which is meant to preside over the whole of our thought, our movement, our instincts and our feeling—this authentic self cannot express itself. The conditions of modern life are especially difficult in this regard. Nowhere is there support for the expression or manifestation of that in ourselves which is beyond time and death. In fact, almost everything that we call "progress" is actually measured by the degree to which it enables us to conduct ourselves without the need to bring thought into conscious relationship with movement or feeling. We measure progress by the automaticity by which we are enabled to conduct our lives. Even thinking, or what is called "thinking," is being performed more and more by machines. These machines are supposed to liberate us—but for what? As has been noted, the net result of all our technological invention has been to take our time away from us. The time of the soul is not the time of the machine. And especially it is not the time of electronic impulses.

The third approach to the idea of the soul can now be understood. Are there moments when, despite our conditioning and cultural environment, the soul actually does express itself? Are there moments when the true self and the social self actually make contact? Moments when the ego, the self that I am in my ordinary life, recognizes the soul? Are there such moments? Moments when two worlds come into relationship—two worlds, two qualities of time, moments when time, and eternity intersect?

THE ARRIVAL

There are such moments.

I am fifteen years old; it is a brilliant October day; flaming maples and oaks line the street; the sky clear, crystalline blue; early morning. I am walking to school. Alone. Cars and trucks are beginning their morning hum. Cool autumn air, pure and sweet on my face and in my nostrils. Suddenly, for no apparent reason, I stop. I stop cold—or so it seems. But my legs continue to move, my arms are swinging rhythmically at my side. Feelings of joy and the fine sensations of my body spread through me and blend like two swift rivers. But my mind—my mind is now slow and calm, moving like an open boat in a quiet lake.

At the same moment, with startling clarity, *I say my name aloud.* I don't recall *intending* to say my name like that, aloud, in strong and even tones—yet the saying of it is filled with intention and will, an intention of a kind I have never known before. I say my name: *Jerry.* And I say, with it: *I am Jerry. I am here. I am alive.*

There is no doubt about this experience. *I am* appeared in me as I was walking that morning. There is no doubt *I am* came from a realm outside of time. It was from *home,* a deeper and more real home than I had ever known. In that moment I was with myself simultaneously as a child, as an infant and as an old man waiting for death. *I am* appeared; it would be more accurate to say: it *arrived.*

And yet *I am* was within time as well. It was moving with me, looking at the trees, the traffic, the street, the people. But it was looking with eyes that served a new purpose. Touched by *I am,* my eyes wanted only to see— they delivered no fear or desire; my ears wanted only to hear, they did not like or dislike; my lungs wanted only to breathe, my lips to taste and speak, my body to move through the ocean of air and time; *I am* wanted to be, simply to *be*. It was born, like an infant, but a different kind of infant, one that craved nothing, feared nothing, but wanted only and purely to look, to see, to exist. It was without desire, yet alive with unbelievable intensity. It arrived—as if to say to me: *Why have you waited so long?* Not accusingly, but uncomprehendingly: why have you waited so long to let me come and be here with you?

And now, it seemed to say, *let me grow!*

And then, gradually, it disappeared. As time passed, as I grew and began my career and found happiness that turned to sadness, triumphs that decayed into anxiety, defeats that became strangely beautiful gifts and openings, like hidden passages through ice and rock, as I made one or two great mistakes in my emotional life— mistakes of the kind that all of us make, mistakes that are really part of our inner structure and that cannot be avoided— as I did my best, as we all do, and saw more and more that my best was not enough, as it never is; as I deceived myself and others about my inner being, as I gathered respect for what I wasn't and enmity for what I wasn't, in short, as my life spun out its thread, these moments of *arrival* came again and again in rare and unpredictable times and conditions. I began to realize my life had meaning only in those moments when I arrived in the midst of my life. I realized more and more that the river of time was taking me nowhere, nowhere but to destruction; but that there was another, a second river, within the broad river of time, like a back-flowing current that one finds near the banks of a deep swift river, and I heard of the idea that one could enter that other current which leads somewhere that is not destruction. And with the help of others who were also searching and who had searched longer than I and who had found the help that the great traditions of wisdom tell us is necessary, I began to search more intentionally and precisely for the source of my being which, as Emerson has said, descends into us from we know not where.

THE GREAT ANSWER

What became clear, and what can become clear for all of us who are starved for time, is that the answer to the problem of time is not more time, not more efficiency, not even in itself longer biological life, not children, not artistic creations that we pretend will bring us immortality, not some sentimental relationship to imaginary gods or non-gods. The answer to the problem and the sorrow of time is one thing and one thing only: *the experience of meaning.* And this experience occurs only when the Self touches the self, when the soul touches the ego. When the two worlds meet.

When the self that is conditioned by society and has learned the language of society is touched by the Self that is beyond society and breathes and lives in wordless reality—that moment is the first step on the great ladder of meaning, the ladder of remembering that is shown to humankind through the wisdom teachings of the world.

It is not necessary to become a mystic, plunging into the luminosity of otherworldliness; nor is it necessary, on the other hand, to become a superefficient ace in the game of "time management." What is needed is the contact between the self that speaks and the Self that is. What is necessary is to realize that it is possible for myself as I am, myself as ego—anxious, nervous, eager to help and to succeed and eager to do my duty to those I love, just that ego who is overwhelmed by life and is always looking for respect and appreciation and rest, that ego who takes his pleasures fitfully and guiltily, who sees time passing more and more rapidly and who feels that life is passing him by without anything ever really happening—just that ego can make contact with the Self. In such a contact, especially if it is repeated and becomes deeper and deeper, and lasts longer, and especially if we have the language and the ideas by which to interpret the experience correctly—such contact can show the ego that what it wants it cannot have by itself, from itself. The contact between the ego and the Self can show the ego that it *is* possible to have love, safety, joy that does not fade, emotion that is based on truth; it is possible to have *time*, an immensity of time, it is possible to be free of fear and false satisfaction—but only through the Self. The Self is everything that the ego pretends to be, and the Self has the time that ego searches for in vain. When these two worlds meet, only then can the ego breathe freely and let go and accept that it is secondary and, yes, mortal. *The ego sees that it does not have to live forever.* It sees this because when *I am* exists the ego has found what it wanted. It, *I,* have found what wisdom calls "the heart's desire."

A NEW KIND OF WISH

Here it would be well to look at the teachings "concealed in broad daylight" in our own Bible. There the passage of time is symbolized everywhere by the image of the *moth.* Job, for example, is reprimanded by Eliphaz to take a surer assessment of man and human life "who dwell in houses of clay, whose foundation is the dust, which are crushed before the moth" (Job 4:19). And in one of the most deeply moving testaments to the way our suffering in time expresses our relationship to the higher forces within and above ourself, the Psalmist cries out:

> Lord, make me to know mine end, and the measure of
> my days, what it is; that I may know how frail I am.
> Behold, thou hast made my days as an handbreadth;
> and mine age is as nothing before thee. . . . And now,
> Lord, what wait I for? My hope is in thee. . . . Remove
> thy stroke away from me: I am consumed by the blow of
> thine hand. When thou with rebukes dost correct man
> for iniquity, thou makest his beauty to consume away
> like a moth. . . . O spare me, that I may recover
> strength, before I go hence, and be no more.[13]

When the self is touched by the Self, the ego sees
where its hope really lies and such moments can become
the beginning of a new kind of valuation, a new kind of
wish or desire that begins to accompany one's everyday
life in the time-starved world. Here, again, the wisdom of
the Western traditions:

> Lay not up for yourselves treasures upon earth, where
> moth and rust doth corrupt, and where thieves break
> through and steal. But lay up for yourselves treasures in
> heaven, where neither moth nor rust doth corrupt, and
> where thieves do not break through and steal. *For where
> your treasure is, there will your heart be also.*[14]

CONCLUSION

"YOU'VE ONLY JUST BEGUN"

Eliot is again in the apartment. I want no ambiguity here: it has *not* been "all a dream." He *has* traveled back in time. As he opens his eyes, the scene is the same as when he left. Through the window behind Max, the October sun is touching the horizon in precisely the same place, and the amber-gold light that fills the room is exactly the same hue and has exactly the same intensity. Had it been a dream, minutes or hours would have passed, the sun would be down, perhaps it would be night. Max would be in a different place, or in a different posture. But everything is precisely the same. It has all taken place between one word and the next, in the space between words, the space between thoughts. It has all been a movement of Eliot's attention, the attention that exists behind and above our thoughts and which we must open to if we seek the Self. This attention, a power of our mind that our modern world does not know about, is not subject to the passing of time.

This attention does not age. The body ages; the capacity of combining and associating thoughts and memories may weaken with time; every system and organ will in time lose its power or break down; the eyes and the ears will lose sensitivity. But attention does not age. We, we who are not aware of attention, who live our lives without understanding that it is the real root of our selves—it is we who age and die, who abandon the inner self, our own essence calling out to us in the desert.

I want to show Max in a way that suggests this ancient knowledge about the nature of attention, that aspect of ourselves that is independent of time as we know it. As was taught in the wisdom schools of antiquity, there is an attention in ourselves that cares for the whole. Plato— putting into words the wordless teaching of his master Socrates—Plato called it the soul. It is a panoramic attention that exists and functions at a different level than what we call attention and what we study under that name.

Max is old, very old. His body is frail, he moves slowly and with difficulty. That body was once rugged and powerful; life poured through it like a many-sourced river. Max had been everywhere and had done everything; those who knew him sensed that he was able in some mysterious way to extract energy from every situation in life; inwardly always calm, yet hugely engaged with men and women, with the labors and perceptions of the body, with health and illness, with knowledge and art, with adventure and risk and the making and losing of money. His life had served the search for the Self and he had helped many others not only to find the Way but to advance along the Way.

And now all that was left of Max was his eyes—that is, his attention, his vision—and his voice, his power to say the necessary word at the right moment. And his physical posture, a stillness of the body in front of which one sensed a fine inner vibration. His silences and his stillness could be felt as "an absence inhabited by a presence." Something remains still in order that something else can move within. Max the "person" and the body that serves the person are approaching death; Max the instrument of Self is vibrantly alive and strong.

And when Max does move—stiffly, in pain; or when he speaks—slowly, sometimes, searching for the words, Eliot senses the conscious attention to the whole that is behind his movements and his words. Even when Max forgets, when he seems to drift off, when he is slow to make a connection of associations, even then Eliot senses the being within him, the result that has accumulated within him of years of inner struggle and service to the search. In a flash Eliot realizes: *This is what it really means to grow old,* and this is what the Bible is saying when it speaks of the great age of the patriarchs and the prophets. Noah was great in years; Jacob was great in years, Solomon was great in years—that is, through their inner

life they had gone beyond time as we know it. This is why
the ancient civilizations, those that had roots in the
teachings of wisdom, revered old age. It was not out of
some sentimentality or some self-serving motive; not out
of a sociopsychological pattern of familial bonding. It was
for a metaphysical reason. An individual who had spent
his life struggling for the inner Self had gathered something within himself that called to every other man or
woman who came in touch with him. In such an old man
or woman *one saw that time was not only a destroyer but a
creator.* And one sensed, as Eliot senses when he is now
with Max, that if something can grow and reveal itself in
this way within a body and a mental apparatus that is fail-
ing under the hand of ordinary time, then it is not only
possible but nearly certain that the source of real life—not
biological life, but conscious life—in a man or woman can
become such as to resist the death of the body itself.

As Eliot opens his eyes, he is given to see and feel this
in Max. He has no words for what he sees. He knows only
that he is seeing his teacher as though for the first time.

Under Max's silent look, Eliot begins to speak about
his experiences in the past. The amber-gold light begins
to darken as the sun drops beneath the horizon. Eliot
starts to turn on a light. "Don't move," Max says gently.
"Keep your position." Soon it is almost too dark to make
out anything in the room. Eliot wants to speak, but he
wants to see Max, he wants to see his face, a face which
he now begins to understand has been made by inner
attention. Eliot waits for his eyes to adjust to the dark.

And, suddenly, a new kind of light appears in the room. A brilliant full moon has risen. As the last traces of dark, golden amber disappears, a silver glow fills the room in its place. And just at that moment Max reaches up to turn on the floor lamp. The artificial light startles Eliot and returns him to the present, ordinary world, the world of ordinary time and ordinary feeling. He realizes that in the moonlight he was entering a kind of dreamy "mystical" reverie. Once again, his old teacher was waking him.

"Talk," says Max. "What have you seen? What have your discovered?"

I know what Eliot has discovered. It is what I am discovering as I struggle with time. This discovery takes the form of a question.

A question that cannot easily be expressed in words, in concepts. It is extremely intimate, extremely close to oneself, closer than one's secret fears and desires. That is why, when Eliot starts to speak of what he has seen of the relationships with Elaine, and with his parents, Max stops him. "It is not interesting," says Max. "Go deeper. Go higher. You were not sent back for that."

Go back in time, back to the beginning, the origin of one's self, one's life. Our modern life in time is drawing us forward, outward toward the future. But it is not our real future; it is not *my* intimate future. Nor is what I call the past *my* intimate past.

Am I living a life that is not my own? Is the stress of time, the famine of time, the result of living a life that is not my own? Could I possibly be driven mad, as we are driven mad, except by a life that is not my own, that is not occupied by my own intimate self, that is not felt and respected in my blood and bone?

Eliot was sent back to witness his life. But he discovers that the witnessing itself is more intimate than what he sees of his actions and what he hears of his words and what he senses directly of the feeling and thoughts of his younger self. He sees that, by being sent back in time, the life he once lived becomes his own through being consciously seen. His life is feeding the witness. And the witness holds back, steps back, watches, tries not to react, but only studies the life that is his life. And in this witnessing a new pulse begins to beat, the heart of a new body, a new life. The older Eliot begins consciously to *feel* his life, consciously to inhabit his existence and his time.

The time of machines is not our own time. Human time is always *my own,* mine, my individual time. Or it is ours, yours and mine. But it is always the time of a being or of beings who can in truth say *I.* In other cultures, perhaps less alienated from the teachings of wisdom, mankind lived in closer relationship to biological time, the pulses and rhythms of nature, the sun and the moon, the tides, the seasons, the light and darkness, all the measures and meters of the music of the earth and the skies. But even this time, this more natural time, is not in itself human time. Human time is always the time of the consciousness that says and means *I, I am.* But to live closer to biological time keeps men and women closer to the possibility of the real *I am* and the real *we are.* The real

individual and the real community. The real indepen-
dence and the real interdependence. To live in accor-
dance with nature's time is to allow the nature that is
within us to beat with more synchronous rhythms—the
body's tempo, the tempos of organic love and fear and
tenderness and anger; and the tempos and rhythms of
the mind that searches, that needs to guide and receive
the action of the senses, to plan and manage and to
remember the gods, the greater forces. Inside each man
and woman nature with its rhythms exists. To live with
these tempos and times more in harmony is to live in the
time of earth and nature and to be a more ready recepta-
cle for the consciousness that can truly say *I am.* Biological time is not in itself human time, but it is closer to it
than mechanical time.

Mechanical time is the time of only one part of our
nature—and only part of the universal world. Through
this mechanical aspect of the world, the world that can be
measured with a watch and then computerized—through
this kind of time the world can be manipulated, the surface world. The whole universal world, however, cannot
be manipulated, never. And by manipulating the surface
world, we—as is now obvious—set up a dangerous imbal-
ance in the whole of nature such that sooner or later, with
inevitable force, nature will be compelled to set the bal-
ance right, with deadly consequences for us and eventually for the earth itself.

We know this about our relationship to the outer
world. But we need also to see that by governing our own

inner world through mechanical, computer time, we are running one part of our nature with a time and a tempo so far removed from the time of our body and our feeling that there is less and less possibility of these central parts of ourselves coming into relationship. And only in the relationship, the actual harmonic contact, between the main sources of perception and energy in ourselves can there be a medium through which the authentic self can appear and act in us. If we look carefully at the moments in our lives when the experience of the Self has been given to us, we will notice that it always takes place when there has suddenly appeared a contact between fundamental aspects of our nature that are ordinarily separated from each other—these aspects being either the mind and the body or the feeling and the mind or the two directions of motivation that constitute the two-natured being, man: namely, the yearning for being and the impulse to action and creation in the world around us.

The problem of time in our world is not due to technology in itself. It is due to the fact that our inner sense of time obeys the machine and acts with the tempo and rhythms of the machine. If we could use the technologies invented by the mind and at the same time retain a relationship within ourselves among all the principal parts of our being, the body, the mind and the feelings, we could make use of technology and still retain our humanness, our real time, our real past and our real future.

Human time is *my* time. But unless "I am," there can be no *my,* there can be no *our.*

It is therefore of little use to long for times past, for more "natural" societies, unless we understand that the heart of all human life is that which allows the God who says "I am" to appear within ourselves. We need only note the horrors that so-called more natural peoples can commit upon each other and even upon nature to disabuse ourselves of a romanticism that sees no further than the connection between man and external nature. The need is for the connection to nature within ourselves; only then can we understand how to act toward nature outside ourselves. Along with the obvious crimes our culture is committing against the natural world, we would be wise to remember that the main crimes are the crimes against our inner nature. From these inner crimes all the outer evil arises.

It is the same with the "crimes" or errors of our own individual private lives. Eliot has been sent back in time to see, to be present in his life exactly as it was and as it is. Through consciously inhabiting the life he has been given, another life begins to grow within him, a life that obeys different kinds of laws, a life where the passage of time means something entirely different. In the second life, the life of evolving attention, the flow of time reverses; a man or a woman comes toward birth even as in the first life time moves us toward death. Birth and death move closer together and finally become one.

Consider—as Eliot is made now to consider under the look of his old teacher: what can actually help us as we spin round ever faster in the inhuman tempo of our lives?

Can we remember the Self while everything about us draws us into forgetting? What can point us to the life within life which defines our humanity? The world we live in knows nothing of the life within life. In this world we are persuaded that we have only one life here and now. It is not so. To be here and now, to fully inhabit the present moment, is to have two lives simultaneously—an inner life and an outer life.

What can actually help us, not so much to slow down, but to exist within ourselves in another kind of time? We may try to change the quality of time—that is, the quality of our outer lives. And we may succeed, in moments, for brief periods, in a normal healthy respite from the inhuman tempo of our culture. But it will only be temporary. What is needed is not the vain effort to change the nature of modern life, to alter the way time flows in our world. What is needed—and what is possible—is to introduce another movement of time within the life we are in fact living. But it is not an effort the ordinary mind can make or even easily understand.

As the novel ends, Eliot is no longer insisting on anything. I want this concluding scene to show that Eliot's time travel has brought him something far different and far greater than he had expected. Instead of discovering new psychological facts about the causes and patterns of his life, he has discovered a new quality of seeing itself. It is not *what* he has seen, it is *that* he has seen which is now of utmost importance. Looking at his old teacher beginning to doze under the fringed floor lamp, Eliot is given to experience something of what Max has been speaking about. He feels free of time because his mind has become absolutely quiet. Within him, as though from behind himself, a fine, subtle presence appears like yet another quality of light, but this time from within himself.

His body is also still and completely relaxed. Without strain or tension, he remains free of time. The presence within him is a completely new person. It is not exactly a consciousness, not exactly a deeper thought, not only a deeper vision or a fine and sensitive current of inner sensing. It is all of these, but first and foremost it is another person. Another person within him. Yet, at the same time, it is *he*. It feels more like himself than he has ever felt before. It is not Eliot. It is not Dr. Appleman. It is *I*. And, suddenly, it becomes *I am*.

It looks out through my eyes, hears with my ears, thinks with my memories and thoughts, understands with my images and feelings, senses with my skin and blood. And it wants nothing more than to see and to be in this life where it is now meant to live. To live and to serve. It is like a baby just born, yet unlike a baby. Its understanding and vision are without violence or impatience. Compared to this newly born I, the adult Dr. Appleman is not even a child, not even born, not even a baby.

Sitting there, watching Max, Eliot understands for the first time what his life is for and what he is meant to obey. At the same time he knows not only that he is seeing something new and real but that, most of all, he is being seen. Not by God above, not by his teacher, not by his own mind and memories or by his knowledge. He is being seen by himself, by the Self that is himself.

This is the Self that is meant to grow in a man or woman. It needs to live and the earth and heavens themselves need it to live and grow. And for that growth there is time, time is given, enough time is given. It is another kind of time and requires another kind of death than the death of the body.

The Way to this new life exists. It can be found. But it must be sought. It is not found in a shop or in a book. But it can be found, because it is looking for us even more than we are searching for it. May we all, every one of us, be found and remembered while . . . while there is still time.

The experience of his own presence lawfully fades away. Eliot sits in his chair for a long time, quietly aware of his calm breathing and the inexplicable happiness within his breast and body. Slowly, he gets up and moves quietly toward the door so as not to disturb Max, who is snoring in his chair, his lion's head bent, his face slack, his arms hanging straight down.

As Eliot opens the door to leave, he is startled to hear a loud animal snorting sound, followed by the voice of his teacher, powerful and steady:

"Appleman, where are you going? Come back. You've only just begun!"

Eliot's heart leaps with joy as he closes the door behind him.

REFERENCES

1. Jeremy Rifkin, *Time Wars* (New York: Henry Holt and Company, 1987), p. 12.

2. Ecclesiastes 3:1–4.

3. *The Dhammapada: The Sayings of the Buddha,* A New Rendering by Thomas Byron (New York: Vintage Books, 1976), p. 3.

4. See especially his *The Sickness Unto Death.*

5. *The Bhagavad Gita,* translated by Juan Mascaró (London: Penguin Books, 1962), Chapter 1.

6. The passages in this chapter are based on the translation by Walter Scott in *Hermetica: The Ancient Greek and Latin Writings Which Contain Religious and Philosophical Teachings Ascribed to Hermes Trismegistus* (Boulder: Hermes House, 1982). Some modification of the text has been made through consulting an anonymous translation made in London and published in San Francisco by Far West Press in 1977 under the title *Hermetica.* In one or two places I have substituted a phrase which seemed more clearly to render the sense of the text.

7. Matthew 6:25.

8. Matthew 6:26–30.

9. Matthew 6:31–34.

10. St. Augustine, *Confessions,* translated by R. S. Pine-Coffin (Harmondsworth, Middlesex: Penguin Books, 1961). Book IX, Section 14, p. 264.

11. Ralph Waldo Emerson, "The Over-Soul." All the citations from Emerson are from this essay.

12. An especially powerful image of the Hindu vision of the idea can be found in the story of "The Parade of Ants" in *Myths and Symbols in Indian Art and Civilization* by Heinrich Zimmer (Princeton: Princeton University Press, 1972), pp. 3–11. The idea of recurrence, as applied explicitly to the paradoxical juxtaposition of free will and predestination in the course of one's life, can be found in the great myth of Er which sounds the concluding chord of Plato's *Republic.* Nietzsche's treatment is developed in *The Gay Science.* As for Ouspensky's compelling vision of this idea, it forms the basis of a great deal of his thought. See his *Tertium Organum* and *A New Model of the Universe* and his novel, *Strange Life of Ivan Osokin.*

13. Psalm 39:4–13.

14. Matthew 6:19–21.

FURTHER
READING

St. Augustine. *The Confessions*. Augustine's reflections on
    time in Book XI have exerted great influence on West-
    ern thought and must be studied by anyone seeking to
    grapple with the question in philosophical terms or
    from a Christian perspective.

Thorleif Boman. *Hebrew Thought Compared with Greek*.
    Philadelphia: The Westminster Press, 1960. An excep-
    tional blend of scholarly precision and philosophical
    imagination, this book clearly and simply illuminates
    the two fundamental and opposed conceptions of time
    that have shaped Western thought. This work is far too
    important to be considered as only for academic
    specialists.

Mircea Eliade. *The Sacred and the Profane*. New York:
    Harper and Row, 1961. And *The Myth of the Eternal
    Return*. Princeton: Princeton University Press, 1954.
    The great scholar of the history of religion argues for
    the radical difference between sacred and profane time.

"Sacred time is indefinitely recoverable, indefinitely repeatable."

Immanuel Kant. *The Critique of Pure Reason.* Anyone who wishes to think seriously about the nature of time is obliged to study the arguments of this great Enlightenment philosopher. His principal book is awesomely difficult and immensely rewarding, and if it is found to be too inaccessible, there exist a number of clear accounts of his teachings—for example, Frederick Copleston's *A History of Philosophy.*

Søren Kierkegaard. *Repetition.* Princeton: Princeton University Press, 1946. Dazzling on the surface, calm and mystically reverent in its depths, this is the great Danish writer's most sustained treatment of the meaning of time.

Lewis Mumford. *Technics and Civilization.* New York: Harcourt, 1934. The classic study, written with great gusto, of the influence of technology on human experience. The first few chapters present startling and important observations about how the invention of the clock influenced the birth of modern science and the spread of world capitalism, thereby creating the modern era as we know it.

Maurice Nicoll. *Living Time.* London: Watkins, 1952. If I had to recommend one title, it would be this one. A life-changing book of great profundity and clarity about the mystery of time, it also unlocks many doors to the inner teachings of Christianity and the spiritual philosophies of the West.

Helga Nowotny. *Time: The Modern and Postmodern Experience.* Cambridge, England: Polity Press, 1994. A brilliant sociopsychological analysis of the relationship between the headlong development of machines and technology and the time crisis of the present age.

P. D. Ouspensky's books offer some of the most powerful and original ideas about time of any twentieth-century philosopher. The whole of *Tertium Organum* (New York: Alfred A. Knopf, 1981) and several essays in *A New Model of the Universe* (New York: Alfred A. Knopf, 1961) offer extraordinary insights. The novella, *Strange Life of Ivan Osokin,* is a spiritually uncompromising story of a man sent back to live his life again.

J. B. Priestly. *Man and Time* (London: Aldous Books Limited, 1964). The best topical overview. A beautifully written personal essay that embraces the historical, scientific, psychological, philosophical and mystical aspects of the subject.

INDEX

ABOUT
THE AUTHOR

Jacob Needleman is professor of philosophy at San Francisco State University. He was formerly visiting professor at Duxx Graduate School of Business Leadership in Monterrey, Mexico, and director of the Center for the Study of New Religions at The Graduate Theological Union in Berkeley, California. Educated in philosophy at Harvard, Yale, and the University of Freiburg, Germany, he has also served as research associate at the Rockefeller Institute for Medical Research, as a research fellow at Union Theological Seminary in New York, as Adjunct professor of medical ethics at the University of California Medical School, and as guest professor of religious studies at the École Pratique des Hautes Études (Sorbonne, Paris).

He is the author of *The New Religions, A Little Book on Love, Money and the Meaning of Life, A Sense of the Cosmos: The Encounter of Modern Science and Ancient Truth, Lost Christianity, The Heart of Philosophy, The Way of the Physician, Time and the Soul,* and *Sorcerers,* a novel. Dr. Needleman also was general editor of *The Penguin Metaphysical Library*, a selection of sixteen reprinted texts dealing with the contemporary search for spiritual ideas and practice; general editor of the Element Books series, *The Spirit of Philosophy*—aimed at repositioning the teachings of the great philosophers of the West to show their relevance to the modern spiritual quest. Among the other books he has authored or edited are *The Tao Te Ching* (Introductory Essay); *Gurdjieff: Essays and Reflections on the Man and His Teaching; Consciousness and Tradition; Real Philosophy;* and *Modern Esoteric Spirituality.* In addition to his teaching and writing, he serves as a consultant in the fields of psychology, education, medical ethics, philanthropy, and business, and has been featured on Bill Moyers' PBS series "A World of Ideas."

His most recent book, *The American Soul: Rediscovering the Wisdom of the Founders,* was published by Tarcher/Putnam in February 2002.